ProACTIVE Selling

Second Edition

Control the Process—**WIN** the Sale

William "Skip" Miller

AMACOM
American Management Association
New York · Atlanta · Brussels · Chicago · Mexico City · San Francisco
Shanghai · Tokyo · Toronto · Washington, D.C.

Bulk discounts available. For details visit:
www.amacombooks.org/go/specialsales
Or contact special sales:
Phone: 800-250-5308
Email: specialsls@amanet.org
View all the AMACOM titles at: www.amacombooks.org

This publication is designed to provide accurate and authoritative information in regard to the subject matter covered. It is sold with the understanding that the publisher is not engaged in rendering legal, accounting, or other professional service. If legal advice or other expert assistance is required, the services of a competent professional person should be sought.

Library of Congress Cataloging-in-Publication Data

Miller, William
    Proactive selling : control the process—win the sale / William "Skip" Miller. — 2nd ed.
        p.   cm.
    Includes bibliographical references and index.
    ISBN-13: 978-0-8144-3192-4
    ISBN-10: 0-8144-3192-5
    1. Selling—Psychological aspects.   2. Relationship marketing.   3. Purchasing—Decision making.   I. Title.   II. Title: Pro active selling.

    HF5438.8.P75M554   2012
    658.85—dc23

                                                        2012007679

About AMA

American Management Association (www.amanet.org) is a world leader in talent development, advancing the skills of individuals to drive business success. Our mission is to support the goals of individuals and organizations through a complete range of products and services, including classroom and virtual seminars, webcasts, webinars, podcasts, conferences, corporate and government solutions, business books and research. AMA's approach to improving performance combines experiential learning—learning through doing—with opportunities for ongoing professional growth at every step of one's career journey.

Printing number
10   9   8   7   6   5   4

Contents

Preface

SELLING. WHAT A PROFESSION. Why do so many people love selling so much, whereas others hate even the *thought* of selling something? What is it about the topic of selling that causes so many mixed emotions? Better yet, why are some people so good at it, and others are always trying to get it right?

> *They say successful salespeople can sell anything. They're right.*
> *They say successful salespeople are born, not made. They're wrong.*

Successful salespeople have five things in common:

1. They think like a customer.
2. They are proactive and always think one step ahead, and therefore they *pull* to control the Buy/Sell process.
3. They have a natural curiosity. They ask. Great salespeople do not have great answers . . . they have great questions.
4. They qualify from a buyer's perspective early and often. Yeses are great, nos are great . . . maybes will kill you.
5. They use the right tool at the right time at the point of attack: the sales call.

This is the second edition of *ProActive Selling*. The tools presented in the first edition have stood the test of time. We've trained hundreds of companies and tens of thousands of salespeople in all industries and all disciplines. The principles in this book apply to all companies, whether the company had a $500 30-minute sales cycle or whether the average sale was more than $1,000,000 and took one to two years to complete. Companies in any domain or industry—hardware, solutions, shoes, software, SaaS, cloud, products, HVAC, services, and so forth—all have something in common: Salespeople who qualify and control the Buy/Sell process usually win the deal.

In the years we've been doing sales and sales management training, we've observed over and over again qualities in sales professionals and the sales tools they use during a sales call that consistently set them apart from the rest of the pack. *ProActive Selling* clearly identifies the tools that successful salespeople use on a daily basis and presents them for salespeople to use to add value in the way they are currently selling. *ProActive Selling* is not another "sales process" book, nor is it about "strategizing a sale." There are too many books out there that define a "new way of selling" or a "new sales methodology." A salesperson will likely get better results using his or her current, "ineffective" way than by using those books.

Believe it or not, *there is no one right way to sell.* There are many different approaches you can take to selling, and they are each very successful in their own right.

However, what we need is a way to improve how we sell on each and every sales call. You need to improve your sales skills and increase the number of tools you use. *ProActive Selling* provides sales tools for the your toolbox so that at the point of attack (i.e., the sales call), you can feel you are fully armed, not just carrying a couple of bullets.

ProActive Selling describes what is going on in the buyer's mind and how you can use this information ProActively. It shows you how to use the right tool at the right time so you can sell more effectively every time you engage with a potential customer.

How Salespeople Sell the Right and the Wrong Way

There is a motto for ProActive salespeople, and it is: Tactics before strategies within a process. It's that simple. Successful salespeople sell in a process. Within that process they should use tactics and then combine them with a sales strategy, rather than strategize an account and then implement tactics. It's important to put the pieces of the process in the right order, tactics before strategies, to be ProActive. Otherwise, the customer controls the sale, and the salesperson is forced into a reactive posture. Putting strategies first makes salespeople reactive. Because their tactics are poor, they are getting poor information in the development of their strategies. Putting tactics first allows the salesperson to gather quality information during a sales call so the strategy part of the sale has complete and competent information.

The number one reason salespeople lose an account is that they are out of control of the sales process. Period. That's worth saying again. The number one reason a sale is lost is because the salesperson is not in control of the Buy/Sell process. Salespeople will always claim the reason they won a deal is because they were *so* smart, and that the reason they lost a deal could be one of a host of other reasons, none of which are in the salesperson's control, of course.

What these salespeople don't realize is that control of the Buy/Sell cycle is the number one factor in determining whether a sale will be won or lost, even above best fit of product or solution. In addition, this control is totally the responsibility of the salesperson. Salespeople must learn the tactics of how to control a sales process to increase their chances for success

As a salesperson, you should feel free to combine the tactics and tools of *ProActive Selling* with any of the strategic sales methodologies you like to round out your selling experience. If you have only a strategic piece of the sales puzzle, and then try to figure out the tactics to go along with it, you may stumble at the point of attack. If you are armed with tactics and the Buy/Sell process along with your own sales strategy, you'll increase your chance of success, dramatically.

In discussions we have had with senior sales management, we found they all want the same things.

1. Shorter sales cycles: Shorten the sales process so more transactions can be made per salesperson.

2. Better forecasts: Better quality and quantity of deals in the pipeline—the ideal is 90+ percent accuracy in the 90-day forecast, rather than the 50 to 60 percent accuracy they deal with today.

3. Elimination of "maybe" or bad deals early in the cycle.

4. Control of the sale throughout the sales process, so value can be sold instead of price.

5. Lower cost of sales while increasing the average selling price (ASP) per order.

6. Implement a sales communication process into the sales organization and the rest of the company.

7. Constantly increase the competencies in the sales team to take the A players to A-plus status.

If you are a sales manager wrestling with these strategic issues day in and day out, and want to help your staff understand how easily they can be dealt with if they focus on the right things, then this is a book for you as well. Instead of spending hours with a salesperson behind the scenes dabbling in account strategies, you now have a better option.

Instead of working out the strategy before you get face to face with the customer, you can have a major impact in all of the above issues if you focus on the tactics of selling and help your sales staff focus on the rule of putting tactics before strategies; it's that straightforward.

ProActive Selling has twenty-seven tools for the salesperson to use during the sales call in order to maintain control of the process. A sales manager can use these same tools to make sure the salesperson is really in control of the sale, at the point of attack, the sales call.

The Two-Dimensional Process of Selling

Most salespeople do not have a sales process. They think they do, but try to have them describe it for you. Most salespeople can't. Without a defined sales process, salespeople can react only passively to customers. Such reactive salespeople base their approach on:

- **Customer selling:** The customer leads the sales process and the salesperson follows.
- **Experience selling:** This is the process of hoping that past experience will lead to future success.
- **Catch-up selling:** The competition directs the sale and then you have to play catch-up all the time.
- **Bad sales manager selling:** The sales manager enforces the "do it like I did" methodology.
- **Situational selling:** Every sales call is "on a wing and a prayer."

There's a process of selling that's more successful than most so-called selling processes. It is two-dimensional; it not only has the selling process covered, but also addresses the buying process. As you will find out in Chapter 1, there is a very specific process in how people buy. Salespeople are drilled on controlling the sales cycle, but without the added dimension of understanding the buying cycle and matching the salesperson's selling process to the buyer's buying process, they will not be in control of the overall sales process.

Traditional Tactics Are Not Enough

Salespeople are given sales tactics early on in their careers. These tactics may have included open probes/close probes, elevator speeches, and closing techniques. These are all good skills, but they're much too elementary for today's sales environment—and are one-dimensional. They can't be combined and leveraged with other skills throughout the life of a sale. Most, if not all, sales efforts today put strategies before tactics. Develop the strategic side of the sale, regardless of what the buyer wants to do, and then push the customer through a one-dimensional sales process. The heck with what the buyer wants to do; push that sales process. This can be a successful approach, but it is very reactionary and is missing the two-dimensional part of selling. It forgets about what the customer wants to do. You can argue that all the homework (strategy) a salesperson does is selling-centric. It focuses on how a salesperson plans for a sales process, regardless of the selling tactics required to accomplish the strategy and align with a buyer/seller sales cycle.

Putting tactics before strategies within a process implies that the salesperson is thinking what is needed for the next step in the *buyer*/seller relationship, and then fitting the tactics into a *buyer's* strategy, which after all is what the buyer is following. What tactics are needed to keep control of the sale and convince the buyer that he or she should follow the salesperson in an atmosphere of mutual discovery, which of course salespeople need to lead? This buying-centric nature of selling, this nonreactionary sales approach, and this buyer-first approach is the core of *ProActive Selling*, since it is all about Buy/Sell tactics that fit into a process.

Finally, *ProActive Selling* works even better the higher up you go in a buying organization. We all know the "trick" of calling high in a customer's organization.

But calling high is not the trick. Anyone can do that. The trick is when you're there, what do you say?

What do you say to have the senior-level executive (CEO, CIO, CFO, COO, etc.) treat the salesperson as a value-add asset and to have the executive stay engaged? How can you avoid the C-level executive sending you down into the bowels of the organization from which it is nearly impossible to get back up?

ProActive Selling addresses not only what salespeople have to say at the CXO (Chief X-*fill in the blank* Officer) level, but gets them comfortable in calling high and staying high, as well as being a value-add to the senior-level executive. *ProActive Selling* is so good at the CXO level that salespeople frequently find the senior executives of the account calling them and asking the salesperson what they should do next.

Tactics before strategies in a two-dimensional selling model is what *ProActive Selling* is all about. It's what makes successful salespeople great. That is, their attitude of:

- Focusing on how people buy, not how you want to sell.
- Focusing on the Buy/Sell process, not just the sales process.
- Looking at the sale as a series of *buyer*-related steps.
- Qualifying early in the process and then deciding if you want to spend time with an account, rather than hoping the buyer wants to spend time with you.
- Taking control and having the buyer follow your lead.
- Closing at the beginning of the process, not at the end. There is no such thing as a great closer, or "great closing skills."
- Having the right tools at the right time for the right call.

By successfully reading and implementing the tactics and processes in *ProActive Selling*, you will be able to:

- Accomplish more in less time.
- Be ProActive and anticipate the next sales step.
- Motivate yourself to call successfully at all levels in the organization.
- Control the sales process. The salesperson who controls the sales process . . . wins.
- Get rid of maybes in your sales funnel.
- Learn where to hunt and use your time most effectively.
- Plan and utilize homework on the sales call.
- Lower the overall cost of sales.
- Increase the average selling price per order.

◆ Create a powerful sales introduction on every sales call.

◆ End every sales call and stay in complete control of the sale.

◆ Understand the buyer's motivational direction.

◆ Master the seven qualification questions to call on the right accounts all the time.

◆ Speak the right language to the right level of buyer.

◆ Change a maybe to a decision easily and effectively. ("Yes" is best, but even "no" sure beats "maybe.")

On a final note, we use the term *prospect* in this book rather freely. When we refer to a "prospect," we mean an individual or a group of individuals who are chartered to make a purchase decision. It could be anyone from an individual buying a new computer to a major corporation working through a committee to make a decision on a new infrastructure automation system. There are many differences at the strategic level between these examples, but the buy process and the tools a salesperson uses during the sales call are easily transferable.

For the most part, selling is selling, so *ProActive Selling* works if you are selling a product, service, or tangible or intangible item. It works when selling over the phone, over the Internet, face to face, or through channels. The examples in the book are simple and easy, but you shouldn't think that *ProActive Selling* is effective only for simple sales situations. The *strategies* of a sale can and do change based on what you are selling, usually based on the size of the order and length of the sales cycle. The tactics and process of a sale rarely change, regardless of the sale size or length of a sale, since it all involves sales calls, which is what *ProActive Selling* is here to make you better at. Good luck, and learn how to better your sales skills. . . . ProActively.

Acknowledgments

IT'S HARD TO THANK EVERYONE who has made *ProActive Selling* so successful; there have been just too many people. From salespeople who have helped with new ideas for tools, to vice presidents and CEOs who have looked at these tools not just as a way to sell, but as effective communication tools and a common language they can ProActively manage.

All the M3 Learning clients have been of major help. Thanks in believing and keeping *ProActive Selling* alive and well. Use the tools.

To AMACOM and all the staff, past and present (Bob and Ellen), thanks for putting up with someone who has no writing skills, but has some ideas of how salespeople can do a better job. Debbie, you took clay and gave it form—thank you. Thanks also to Mike Sivilli and all the people who shepherded this manuscript into print.

To the M3 Learning and M3X staff, who have been great and are always one step ahead of me.

To my family, thank you for all the support, love, and understanding. I could not have a better one. Alex, Brianna, and Kyle; all the time. Susie, you're the best.

Nancy and Tom, we miss you.

CHAPTER 1

ProActive Selling: Having the Right Tools at the Right Time to Be a Step Ahead

IT WAS THE END OF AN IMPORTANT MEETING. Brad had spent weeks getting this meeting together so he and his company could be included in the client company's evaluation. He had just made a presentation to the customer's senior management team and was very pleased with how it went.

> *"Brad, this looks very, very interesting to us,"* the senior vice president said, *"and we like what we see. Why don't you call on Kurt and Seline, who are heading up this selection, and start working with them? They have been at this for a few weeks, and you should be considered along with the other people we are looking at right now."*

Brad is certainly excited. He is happy with the way the presentation went, and the senior vice president is now telling him what he should do next. This follows the old sales rule that if you just do what the prospect tells you to do, and you do it well, then the order will follow. Right? Wrong!

If Brad does what the senior vice president wants him to do, he loses

1

control of the sale, which puts him at a disadvantage. Remember the Law of Sales Control.

THE LAW OF SALES CONTROL

The buyer is *always* neutral. If you are not in control of the sale, and the buyer is neutral, then someone else is in control, and it is usually the competition. (And that competition could be an alternate choice of action, such as to do nothing, spend the money elsewhere, delay the process, or even another competitor. Anything that prevents you from getting an order is competition.)

Brad needs to stay in control of this meeting (and we give you a tool, Summarize, Bridge, and Pull^(Tool), that will help you do exactly this; see Chapter 5). He has to identify the next step and have the customer agree to it, not just do what the senior vice president tells him to do. Senior executives want to be guided just like lower level people in the buyer's organization. They just give you very little time to take control, since they are used to having it. They will give up control, however, if you have a planned-out next step that makes sense to them and is seen as helpful to them.

"Mr. Henry, that's a very good idea, bringing Kurt and Seline into this process. It sounds like we have had a good meeting today. You've stated your desire to increase capacity by 10 percent in your current channels while keeping costs constant. You've also stated you want to have a solution in place by the end of the year. We have brought to light some solutions that may be very appealing, so I think we have had a good meeting today, would you agree?"

"Yes, I would say so."

"Great. A good next step then would be for us to get together with Kurt and Seline to really dig into the business issues that are driving you right now on this decision, as well as getting together with you to discuss the overall risks to you and the business strategy by the end of next week. You will then be in a good position from a technical as well as a financial perspective to make a decision if you should continue to go forward with this process. Does this sound like a good next step to you?"

By using the Summarize, Bridge, and Pull tool, Brad stayed in control of this sale. He has now been ProActive, not reactive, and has increased his chances of getting this sale.

Tool-Based ProActive Selling

What happened here? What went on during this sales call? Isn't it common for a salesperson to get excited during a sale when the customer gives direction on what to do next, especially if it is a senior manager? All too often, the best sales strategy is planned out before the call, and then during the sales call, the salesperson makes a mistake and loses control. If Brad does what the senior executive asked him to do, that is, talk to Kurt and Seline next, Brad will be spending much more time adjusting the sales strategy with his sales manager than building his selling tactics around the new strategy. He will be in a reactive sales mode and will be hoping that the customer selects him and his company as the winning vendor. He will also be hoping to see the senior manager again at some time during the process. Hope is a good thing, but not in sales. Putting strategies in front of tactics results in merely hoping for a good outcome, and is the wrong approach.

Instead of just hoping for the best, salespeople need to develop a toolbox of selling tools, so that when they make their pitch, they can execute their sales tactics flawlessly. The strategic part of selling comes later.

Brad used the Summarize, Bridge, and Pull tool as a tactic to keep the Buy/Sell process under his control. By mastering his sales tools, Brad was able to keep this deal alive and own the Buy/Sell process.

When all is said and done, the salesperson who owns the process owns the deal. Keeping in control of the process is the hard part, especially if you don't have the tools to do the job correctly. *ProActive Selling* has twenty-seven sales tools that you can use during the sales call to establish, recover from, and maintain control of the sales process. These will help you to increase the chances a deal will go your way and minimize the chances you will hear a no, or worse, a maybe.

The Customer's Perspective

Successful salespeople understand the buyer's as well as the seller's perspective. They understand that the most critical element in a sale is the prospect, since the prospect is the one who is placing the order, will be using the product/service, and will be paying for it. It's the buyer's value proposition, not the salesperson's value proposition, that is really important.

Buyer's Value Proposition

So what exactly is this "buyer's value proposition"? It's a statement of promised benefits the customer is going to get by using your product or service to create value for *their* customers. This might be the most important thing you learn in this chapter.

If you can't address the prospect's value position, your sales message will be loaded down with information the buyer is not interested in.

Here are some examples of poorly constructed sales messages that center around the "salesperson's value proposition":

"It is very important for us right now to succeed. For us to make that happen, the customer needs to understand our new value proposition."

"We have to be extremely clear in our value proposition to our potential clients."

"We have to lead with our value statements, then get into the rest of the presentation."

Have you ever heard anything so one-sided? The truth is, prospects couldn't care less about your value proposition. What they care about is *their* value proposition—the value they are supplying to *their* customers.

If you take the perspective of the customers in the value proposition theory, you will find out how your product or service will help make them money and help them become more competitive. The real value proposition is taking the prospect's perspective of value they need to supply to their customers, as well as yours.

The USB 3.0 Cable Theory

It's like when you start to work for a new company. You really want to know about what you're going to sell.

So the company (typically the marketing department) sticks a USB 3.0 cable in your head, and proceeds to download all the features and benefits about the company and what it sells. Product features and benefits, competitive advantages, product road maps, and the like. You get excited, really excited, so you ask your company:

"Excuse me, can I borrow this cable? If I get so excited about the company and what we do with this 3.0 cable, I am sure my customers will get excited in the same way."

You then go to your prospects, armed with your USB 3.0 cable, and find out they don't have a 3.0 USB slot.

Customers buy for what your products and services will do for *them*, not for what they actually do—and certainly not because these products or services get *you* excited or make you feel proud.

So just leave that USB 3.0 cable back at the company when you go on sales calls. What excites you about working for the company is not the same reason customers will buy from you.

The buyer's perspective in the Buy/Sell process is the key missing element in most sales processes. It's vital that you understand the perspective of the prospect as well as the seller. This is the basic sales premise you will start with, and then learn ProActive sales tools to assist you in controlling that process.

What Is a Buy/Sell Process?

As you read this book, you will find that the Buy/Sell sales process is different from what you may be used to, since we are asking you to think like a buyer as well as a seller.

So, just for a moment, forget everything you know about how you should sell. Forget about selling methodologies, selling processes, or how you go through a sales cycle. Instead, think like a buyer.

A little reflection shows there is a process in how people buy. If you can define that process, you can understand where a prospect is headed and what steps they are taking to get there. Because you know where the prospect is going, you can then be a step ahead and pull the prospect through their buying process. You can control the prospect's buying process. You don't have to guess at all.

If you understand the process of how a prospect moves to a purchase decision, you can be ProActive. You can be a step ahead and pull the prospect to the next step along the way—pulling, not pushing, the sale. When you pull, you are in control. When you pull, you are pulling the control to you. When you push, you wind up pushing control away. And remember, no one likes a pushy salesperson—ever!

A prospect goes through a number of different steps in a buying process (see Figure 1-1), each with its own unique set of requirements.

Step 1: Initial Interest

The first step in the buying process is for prospects to have an Initial Interest.

People can be interested in many things.

"I'm interested in buying a new car."

"I'm interested in a new TV."

"I need to buy a new machine for the factory floor."

"I am interested in looking at a consulting service right now."

"I need an answer to a current problem I have."

Although important, interests are not enough for the buyer to make a purchase or actually to do something. It's when the prospect is motivated to do something about that interest that he or she starts a buying process. Motivation is the difference between being interested

Figure 1-1 The Buyer's Buy/Sell Process

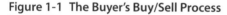

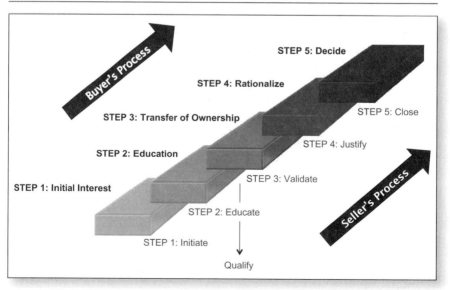

and needing or desiring something; it has motion, and it starts to have a life of its own. Motivation is the prospect's reason for taking action. Initial Interest is more than just interest; it is motivation driving a need or desire.

A motivated prospect will start some action, but how can you motivate a prospect? How motivated is the prospect to begin with? How can you get a prospect to see she has a need for what your product or service can do for her?

Salespeople use several "sales" techniques to motivate their clients to buy:

- ♦ Find the pain.
- ♦ Press their hot button.
- ♦ Instill fear, uncertainty, and doubt (FUD factor).
- ♦ Appeal to value and Return on Investment (ROI).
- ♦ Identify the real need.
- ♦ Have them understand the value proposition.

It's hard to argue with these techniques, but they don't adequately address a buyer's motivation.

There are two motivators that affect human behavior: pain and pleasure. Therefore most people, and buyers *are* people, orient their behavior around the avoidance of pain or the obtainment of pleasure.

In sales, you are really not interested in motivation per se, since by itself, without a need, motivation is stagnant and has no time definition or motion, two critical elements of selling. So motivation with a need is still not very useful to a salesperson without a time and motion element. What is useful to a salesperson is motivational direction.

Motivational direction directly addresses the pain/pleasure motivation of a prospect. It covers the avoidance part of pain, which we will call AWAY, and the attainment part of pleasure, which we will call TOWARDS. TOWARDS and AWAY are what salespeople are really interested in during the Initial Interest part of the buy process (see Figure 1-2).

TOOL **TOWARDS/AWAY**Tool

Prospects are either "TOWARDS buyers" or "AWAY buyers." For the most part, this is absolute. They tend either to move away from pain or towards pleasure, and how they are motivated affects their buying

Figure 1-2 Buyer Motivations

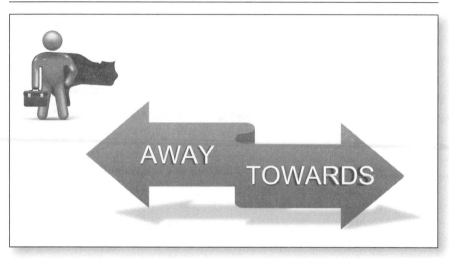

patterns. How do you find out whether someone is a TOWARDS or AWAY buyer? Listen to what they tell you.

AWAY buyers will always have that negative spin. They will tell you what motivates them is the avoidance of something. When asked a question like, "Why would you buy a new TV?" AWAY buyers would respond:

> *"The old one just isn't working right."*
> *"It doesn't have the features on it I need."*
> *"It doesn't interface to the Internet."*
> *"My old one is pretty well shot."*
> *"I am tired of looking at such a small screen."*

All focused on the negative part of the sale. AWAY people are moving away from something, usually away from some sort of pain.

> "I am an AWAY buyer. Don't tell me how great something is, or how much more use I will get out of something, because I do not care! I will agree with your logic, but it will not motivate me. Tell me what I can't have, won't get, or will lose by not having, and you have my attention."

The prospect who is a TOWARDS buyer would have a very different reaction to the same question.

"I like the new features."
"I like the looks of it."
"It will fit great in my living room."
"I want to watch my movies on a big screen."
"I want to feel the action in my living room."

There's nothing negative about their responses. Instead, they identify all positive, forward-moving reasons, and this marks the characteristics of a TOWARDS buyer. They don't express any thoughts on the previous product, but rather focus on the desirable features of the new one.

"I am a TOWARDS buyer. I have to have the latest, coolest thing. My old one . . . geez, let me think . . . I don't even remember if I have an old one."

There is one other type of buyer who tries to evade the question. When asked, "Why would you want a new TV?" these buyers respond with comments like:

"I just want one."
"I need one."
"I don't know, I just have to have one."

For this type of buyer, you need to ask again gently, "Why would you really buy one? When it comes down to it, why would you buy a new TV?" They usually then really search their feelings and tell you their reasons. Nine times out of ten, they will give you an AWAY reason.

Here's a story from my own life that perfectly illustrates AWAY motivation.

Many years ago, I had an old Mercedes Benz. It was well over ten years old, and I was thinking about getting a new car. People would come up and tell me about new features certain cars had, and how one car had a new this or a new that, and I really agreed with their logic. Even so, I was not motivated to do anything about it.

Then one day, my brother came up to me and said I needed a new car. I assured him I was looking but had not seen a reason to buy something other than what I already had. His comment to me was that I should not care about those other reasons either.

The reason he offered for why I should buy a new car was that the car I owned was starting to look old, and quite frankly, *I* was starting to look old in that old car.

Me? Looking old? In my car?

I started to drive past retail store windows to see if in fact the car was starting to look old, or if I was starting to look old in the car. It didn't matter what I thought; the damage was done. I didn't want to start looking old in an old car! Within thirty days, I bought a new car.

Psychologically, between 70 and 80 percent of the world's population is AWAY. One hundred percent of your company's sales literature is TOWARDS. It's no wonder that the TOWARDS sales literature that pronounces the latest and greatest features and functions about your product or service quickly becomes trash basket fodder for senior salespeople. But if sales and marketing people tell customers what they won't get, can't have, can avoid doing—they will get the attention of 70+ percent of the audience.

Sales Literature "Direction" Words

TOWARDS	AWAY
Great	Stop
New	Avoid
Improve	Less
40 percent better	Before it's too late
Act now	Prevent

Although the vast majority of your prospects are AWAY buyers, don't forget to also find the pleasure (TOWARDS). Twenty percent of the buyers are TOWARDS, early adopters, and they have no concept of "finding the pain." They have a vision, a mission, a path they are on, and they need those TOWARDS reasons. You want to be able to sell to buyers with both types of motivational direction.

Additionally, when buyers transfer ownership (see Chapter 10, Validate), they need TOWARDS reasons to do so. TOWARDS reasons and statements do have a place with AWAY buyers . . . just not in Step 1: Initial Interest.

PLAY THE ODDS TIP: If 80 percent of buyers are AWAY at the Initial Interest stage, then make sure you have more AWAY words and questions than TOWARDS words and questions in your e-mails, voice mails, and introductions at prospecting meetings. Place these words by your phone so you have access to these buyer motivational drivers.

> ## AWAY Words
>
> ◆ bring to an end/stop/close/standstill, end, halt
>
> ◆ finish, terminate, discontinue, cut short, interrupt, nip in the bud
>
> ◆ deactivate, shut down, reduce, make less/smaller, minimize, decrease
>
> ◆ allay, assuage, alleviate, keep down, keep at/to a minimum, cut down, lessen, curtail, diminish, prune, slash
>
> ◆ attenuate, palliate, ease, dull, deaden, blunt, moderate, mitigate, dampen, soften, tone down, dilute, weaken

Why is this important? Because, you'll never guess what customers are trying to do. They are not trying to buy your products or solution, that's for sure. You want to know what they are trying to do? Ready? OK, here goes—customer's mission statement!

> ## CSP—Customers Solve Problems
>
> If the customer does not have a problem, you have no deal, period. It's that simple. If the prospect does not have a driving problem (motivation) in the area you are discussing, there probably won't be any action taken for the foreseeable future, since they have a host of other problems they are trying to solve.

Buyers are interested in many things. Based on how they prioritize and are motivated over time, their motivational direction to do something about it will determine whether their interest level is high enough for them to continue their movement and to go to the next phase, called Educate.

Step 2: Education

Buyers, if they are motivated past the Initial Interest phase, will then want to educate themselves on what they can do to satisfy the initial need they have developed. Salespeople usually respond with Feature/Benefit or Feature/Advantage/Benefit selling techniques. There are, however, two levels to the Education step.

The first level is the Technical Case/User Buyer level, which is the level of buyer to which most salespeople sell. This is the buyer who wants to really understand what you are selling; they are the ones who are going to be using it, praising it, and complaining about it—and they have been put in charge of making sure the company "gets its money's worth" on the investment. The User Buyer is under immense pressure. They are given a "budget," told to stay within it, and then must select something that is going to solve a problem—or they won't be receiving the funds to make the purchase.

Technical Case/User Buyers will be pushing you hard on what you offer, what you sell, how you sell it, and how you package it. They'll read every page of your proposal. That's their job and they want to make the best selection they can for their own benefit as well as the company's.

The Business Case level is all about money. This buyer is focused on what metrics—soft dollars, hard dollars, ROI—by which the company measures success.

In Chapter 2, you will see in more detail how you have to sell to both of these levels to be successful.

Step 3: Transfer of Ownership

Now comes the most interesting part of the buyer's process. Here the buyer either gets on board or stops the buying evaluation. This is where the buyer takes ownership of the solution being offered, decides to stay in the education mode, or stops the evaluation altogether. Welcome to Transfer of Ownership.

The best way to describe this is there is a difference between when a buyer first says "I get it," and when, later, they really say "I get it."

The first "I get it" is when the buyer fully understands your product, its features, and its solution. They know what you are offering, the features and the benefits.

The second "I get it" is when the buyer starts thinking how they are going to use it. How they are going to install it, start working with it, how their life will be easier, they will be able to make more money, etc. This is called transfer of ownership, or validation.

All salespersons know when transfer of ownership takes place because they have been in sales situations in which the buyer "gets it." The buyer now understands how he would be able to use the product or service being offered and agrees with the benefits (what's in it for me [WIIFM]).

Every salesperson has experienced this feeling of transfer of ownership, this moment when the prospect says,

> "OK, I get it now. If I buy this service/product and implement it this way, then I will be able to do this and that, and then I will really start saving money on . . ."

The customers start selling themselves. It is what every salesperson dreams will happen on every sales call. The prospect gets it and now is pushing you on how fast something can be done. The pressure is now on the salesperson to follow through.

First "I Get It"	Second "I Get It"
I see how it works.	I see how we are going to solve the problem of . . .
It looks good.	I see where it fits into our plans.
I understand how it works.	I understand how we can install it next week.

With the first "I get it," the prospect is acknowledging they are educated. They see what your product/service does. They see how it works and understand how it functions. They get it.

With the second "I get it," they take ownership. They are actually stopping to think how what you are selling is going to save them time, mitigate risk, and make them money. They have figured out how they are going to use it and they see it in operation.

Transfer of Ownership (a.k.a "validation") must occur for a prospect to continue on in their buying process. It happens, however, in one of two ways. Either the prospect takes ownership of the product/service themselves, or they are ProActively induced into taking ownership. Either they figure it out on their own, or the salesperson has helped them figure it out. The first way is reactive. The prospect is reacting to information, and then on his or her own finally gets it.

The second way is ProActive. The salesperson has helped lead the buyer through the Transfer of Ownership stage. He or she has ProActively induced the transfer of ownership in the buyer's mind. If transfer of ownership happens through the first way, the salesperson was simply lucky. If it happens through the second way, the salesperson was good.

THE LAW OF BEING LUCKY
RATHER THAN GOOD

"I'd rather be lucky than good" . . . nah . . . I'd rather be good, because it is repeatable and leveragable. I can recreate success over and over again.

Be a good salesperson so you can be ProActive in the right situation at the right time again and again and again. How do salespeople ProActively induce transfer of ownership?

As a first example, let's say you are interested in buying a pair of shoes. Either your old ones are getting pretty bad (AWAY), or there are some new ones you really desire (TOWARDS). Whatever the motivation direction may be, you have an interest in a pair of shoes. The interest is so high that you take time to educate yourself on shoes. You may look in a catalog, a fashion magazine, or at other people's feet; you may actually go down to the store and window-shop. If your motivation is still high at this point, and you see a pair that may be of some interest to you, you pick up the display sample, find a salesperson, and say, *"Can I please see these in a size X?"*

Now the store clerk goes away for a few minutes, and comes back with the pair of shoes you want to try on. Then you make a decision, yes or no, on this particular pair of shoes. This is a typical shoe selling experience. If the salesperson was ProActive, he came back with not just the pair you asked to see, but with two or three additional pairs of shoes for you to try on. Why would a salesperson take so much time in the back room, risk losing you because you don't like to wait, to bring you out a pair of shoes you have requested, and two or three pairs you did not request? Good salespeople know their job is not to sell you shoes; it is to get you to try them on. They know once you have a pair of shoes on your feet, they have a better chance at a sale than if you did not take some physical action and get involved. Good shoe salespeople are not wasting time; they are just trying to increase their odds at getting a sale. Good shoe salespeople are ProActive and can ProActively induce the transfer of ownership.

As a second example, a software company has just given an hour demonstration to a client. The demonstration was set up to transfer ownership, not just to educate. The salesperson is a ProActive one. The meeting is about to adjourn. All she has to do is give a final closing summary, have the software engineer say a few final words, and then propose a next step. You might think that the demonstration, or transfer of ownership in this case, was the 45 minutes or so the software engineer had the customers in front of the computer screen. They asked some questions, the salesperson answered them, and things looked good. They seemed to really understand the software. The salesperson might make the mistake of offering as the next step a proposal to keep this sale moving. Instead, now is the perfect time to complete the transfer of ownership. The salesperson, before the final summary and proposal to go to the next step, stops and turns to the customer and says,

> "Based on what you have seen today, let's assume you had a system like this successfully up and running for six months now. What decisions would you be making now? What other decisions would you be making knowing you had the right information this system provides?"

The conversation is now completing the transfer of ownership in the clients' minds. The salesperson is using the TimeDemo^{Tool}, a transfer of ownership tool described in Chapter 10. Instead of the salesperson pushing, the clients are talking about how the system will solve their problems. They are thinking about how they could make decisions on important business issues they cannot make now since they do not have this type of information available to them.

Transfer of Ownership is the buyer's step most salespeople skip. They very incorrectly assume it is part of the education step. You will find out in Chapter 10, Validate, how Transfer of Ownership happens and how to master this step.

Step 4: Rationalize

Once the buyer has completed the transfer of ownership, a unique thing happens. He starts to think:

"Is this the right time to make a decision like this?"
"Have we looked at enough options?"
"Is this the right tool for us or should we look at a few more?"

Funny things happen when buyers are in the Rationalize phase: They come up with objections, they get cold feet, they develop buyer's remorse, they get stuck at the final step, and, perhaps worst, they go to Maybeland.

Salespeople do not anticipate the buyer having to go through a final rationalization process. But buyers do. After a great demonstration, salespeople are eager to put together a final proposal, get it approved, and have the customer sign it ASAP. Reactive salespeople think like this because this is how salespeople generally have been taught to think. However, it is not how a buyer, or a ProActive salesperson for that matter, thinks.

After completing a transfer of ownership and proceeding up the decision path, buyers need one more final justification, one more rationalization. This happens all the time. You try the shoes on one more time. You are ready to buy the shoes, but want to try both on, just to be sure. You are ready to buy the car, but want to look at it one more time before the salesperson comes back with the final papers. Executives call a final meeting with the people who are in charge of using the product or service to make sure, one more time, that they are "doing the right thing" by investing the company's resources and the executive team's reputation. Just as you may want to sleep on a decision overnight just to straighten out your thoughts, the buyer needs this final justification experience, their final rationalization.

Sometimes the buyer breezes through this phase; sometimes it takes a long time and can most definitely kill a deal if it "hangs" in this stage too long without progress. It seems the larger the sale, the more time a buyer spends in this stage. However, buyers who stay in the Rationalization phase too long tend to see the proposed solution now as too old or not current, or, after having slept on it, still cannot make a decision, so was it really right the first time?

When this happens, salespeople say things like:

The buyer:
Has hidden objections
Got cold feet
Has buyers' remorse

The deal:
Seems headed south
Has an echo
Went dark

Has final objections   Went ghost
Is stuck at the final step   Is in Maybeland

Buyers need to rationalize a purchase before they make a final decision. The ProActive salesperson is aware of this step and uses ProActive tools to stay in control of the sale.

Step 5: Decide

The actual decision is the final buying step. If a buyer has gone through the buying cycle and is still motivated, they will make a decision. It will be either yes or no. It is that simple. The buyer decides yes or no, not "Should I sign this order today?" This is very different from what we learned, that closing means "getting an order." Getting an order is a "selling" mentality, and buyers really dislike being "sold to."

The *ProActive Selling* definition of "closing" is obtaining a decision, either yes or no, *without delay*. Yeses are great, nos are great (for different reasons); it's the maybes that will kill you. Time (the "without delay") is the enemy here, and here is where most salespeople make the biggest mistake.

"I just need to polish up my closing skills."

"I can sell. I just need to add a few more closing skills in my repertoire."

"I do everything right, then things fall apart at the close."

"My boss says I am just afraid to ask for the order, but I am asking for the order.

It's just not coming in yet."

As you will learn in *ProActive Selling*, there are really no good "closing skills." There are some negotiating skills you can use in this or any step of selling, but if you are looking for those great closing skills, or even great "trial" closing skills, you will not find them here. Buyers don't "close." They make decisions based on the buying process that has just been described. So the skills you will learn about in Chapter 12, The Skill of Closing the Deal, will be focused on having the buyer feel like the close of a deal is just the final step in a natural buying process. There are no high-pressure (money-losing) tactics here, just some tools to help the buyer through the final step of his buying process.

Matching the Sell Process to the Buy Process

Throughout *ProActive Selling*, you will use the buy process, match it to the sell process, and see how you can always be in control of the sale. Own the process; own the deal.

The buyer's Buy/Sell process was shown earlier in Figure 1-1. The seller's process (see Figure 1-3) appears quite similar, but since the perspective is different, we have given the steps different names. A buyer goes through the following steps.

- Initial Interest
- Education
- Transfer of Ownership
- Rationalize
- Decide

A seller goes through the same steps, but they call them different names.

- Initiate (= Initial Interest)
- Educate (= Education)
- Validate (= Transfer of Ownership)
- Justify (= Rationalize)
- Close (= Decide)

Since this book is for selling purposes, we will call the phases by their selling names, but the buying names are just as applicable.

If you own the process, you own the deal and win the sale. It is very true that people buy from people they like and trust. It's important to improve rapport building and communication skills so that you convey trustworthiness, but it is more important to concentrate on leading the process so that you will own the deal.

Think like a buyer and match your sales process to the buyer's buying process. If you are ProActive and really work the sale from the buyer's perspective, you take the guesswork out of the equation. You know where the buyer is going. You know the buying steps he will be taking, and you don't have to wait for the buyer to "make up his mind" during the sale. You know where he is going and can suggest the next step he should take. If you work a sale this way, you are a ProActive salesperson who will be in control and a step ahead—always.

Figure 1-3 The Seller's Buy/Sell Process

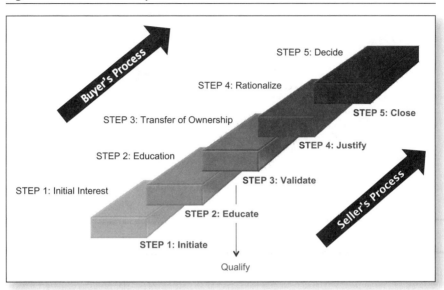

The Length of a Sales Cycle

Before you get into the steps of the Buy/Sell process and into the *ProActive Selling* tools, a word needs to be said on the length of a sale. Some sales cycles are days in duration. Some are minutes. Most sales, however, are measured in weeks and months. What seems to be the gating factor in determining the length of a sales cycle are investment, risk, and sales competencies. Investment and risk are issues for both the buyer and seller. Sales competencies, however, are on the selling side only.

If the investment and risk of a decision are low to the buyer and to their organization, buyers will tend to hurry up their process. If the investment and risk are high, they will tend to take a longer time, since more people and departments are usually involved in the purchase. Risk and investment are not joined at the hip. If risk is high and the investment is low, a decision can still take a long time, and it is also true when the investment is high and the risk is low. Selling organizations balance investment and risk decisions all the time as well to determine if the reward of the sales is worth the time risk investment.

Sales competencies, however, are something the salesperson and sales organization have control over. By improving your selling competencies, you can affect the desired outcome and shorten your sales cycles.

Buy/Sell cycles are usually twice as long as they need to be. If a sales cycle is typically three to four months in your organization, you should be able to eliminate 50 percent of this time. How can you be sure of this?

1. Good salespeople are already doing this.
2. With control of the Buy/Sell process, the delays and slips go away.
3. Since you are in control, the competition is at a disadvantage and is marching to your time schedule. (You know this to be true since you have been on the other side of this phenomenon.)
4. Transfer of ownership has been completed and is anchored to your solution.
5. The buyer has seen the value and knows it is costing them a lot by delaying.

The salesperson usually stretches out the deal. Instead of saying to the prospect, *"Let's get together tomorrow,"* they say, *"Let's get together next week,"* usually doubling the amount of time needed between steps of the sale. Salespeople don't want to appear pushy, so they lengthen the time between meetings. They don't want rejection so they give the buyer all the time in the world.

Buyers want to continue the momentum they have going to make a decision, but are slowing up the process because of the salesperson. *Hmmmmm.*

SALES DELAYS—THE LAW OF 2X

Salespeople take twice the time they need to make a sale.

The salesperson says, *"Let's talk next week."* By doing that, they feel safe and not pushy. From the buyer's perspective, buyer momentum is being lost. They want to speed up the process, but you are the one delaying. The Law of 2X says salespeople should always halve the time they usually wait to present the next step.

> A good friend of mine, Stu Schmidt, says there are only two ways to shorten a sale. Shorten the length of a sales call, or eliminate days in between sales calls or sales touches. Obviously the latter is more beneficial.

You can shorten your sales cycles by increasing sales competencies that control the process. You need to control the Buy/Sell process tactically, within the process, and then update and implement your sales strategy. It is these tactics, these ProActive tools, that you will be using within the Buy/Sell process that will make you a ProActive salesperson.

Why Follow a Process?

You follow a process because it's all about direction. The buyer is progressing through a process, and you can choose to lead, follow, or get out of the way. Buyers need direction with their process. You can provide this direction and add value to their process, especially at the higher levels within an organization.

If you have confidence in the process and the ability to lead and provide direction, buyers will follow you. You will be in charge, you will have a plan and a process, and the confidence you project is contagious. Without a process, the buyers are left to their own devices, and as we discussed before, a buyer is always neutral. They want to be led, and led through a process. Make sure your process mirrors the buyer's process, so it will feel very natural for a buyer.

Mastering the Buy/Sell process will shorten your sales cycles, provide you with control, and give you direction throughout the sale. Without it, a salesperson is at the whim of the buyer, or worse, the competition. Learning and practicing the Buy/Sell process, and applying the ProActive tools you are about to learn, will result in a fully armed and competent salesperson.

CHAPTER 2

The Buy/Sell Cycle Differences

THERE ARE MAJOR DIFFERENCES between how buyers buy and how salespeople sell (although there are certain similarities as well). You may want to take into consideration these differences before you look at the Buy/Sell process.

The two major differences between the two cycles—buying and selling—are:

1. Feature/Benefit/Value Selling^{Tool} (used on the Seller's side only)
2. The Split (occurs on the Buyer's side only)

Recognizing the need to address The Split early and using the FBV tool properly—and being ProActive in your sales approach—will go a long way in making you a better salesperson.

Feature/Benefit/Value Selling vs. Feature/Benefit Selling

| TOOL | Feature/Benefit/Value^{Tool} |

One of the main differences in the Buy/Sell process is how salespeople want to sell, and how buyers want to buy. There are three levels of sales approaches:

1. Feature Selling
2. Feature/Benefit Selling
3. Feature/Benefit/Value Selling

A good salesperson needs to know the differences and which approach to apply in a given situation.

Level One: Feature Selling

Salespeople typically sell with features. Armed with all the product features, they go on and on about what they offer.

"It's the newest . . ."
"It's the smallest . . ."
"It has no competitive rival . . ."
"With our new MD-60 feature, you will just love how it works . . ."
"Our analyst has twenty years of experience . . ."

Most of us have found ourselves in situations with a client where we really can't help ourselves, and we just start spewing all the good things the product/service does. Even I have done it on occasion.

Happily, most of us actually get to the next level in short order.

Level Two: Feature/Benefit Selling

Feature/Benefit selling is just what it sounds like. It describes a feature of the product, then talks about its benefit to the customer, who is typically the User Buyer.

"This is our newest feature, and that will mean 20 percent less work for you."

"Is is now half the size it used to be, so you won't need those special tools anymore."

"It now comes in forty more colors, so you won't be limited in your selections anymore."

The list goes on and on. Feature/Benefit (FB) selling is what happens in over 90 percent of all selling. It can be very effective when:

♦ You are selling to the User Buyer.

♦ There are no Business Case Buyers in your audience.

Now we come to the next level, which most salespeople swear they do, and believe they do well.

Level Three: Feature/Benefit/Value Selling

During the sales education process, ProActive salespeople subscribe to the rule of Feature/Benefit/Value (FBV) selling, since this is the selling language of calling high. FBV states that for every feature you toss out to the prospect, you must have a benefit *and a value* for the buyer, a WIIFM.

"We have a new level of premium service (feature), and what this means to you is between 20 and 30 percent quicker response to your problems (benefit), saving you up to 10 percent of your current costs (value)."

"Our new product is 20 percent faster (feature), which means up to 35 percent less time your people will be spending waiting for the machine to get started (benefit), saving you 10 percent overall in manufacturing costs this year (value)."

"By allowing you access to this new service (feature), you will be able to get your product to market in one-third of the time (benefit), and with 10 percent less risk (value)."

FBV differs from FB selling since it allows the salesperson to sell effectively to more senior executives. FB is selling to what User Buyers want to hear. There is no need for any value statements, since they are not interested in value. On the other hand, FBV allows you and Business Case Buyers in upper-level management to share in the presentation. Keep the focus on the prospect, since you're talking about their value and their WIIFM.

Feature/Benefit	Feature/Benefit/Value
User Buyer	Business Buyer
What they use it for	How it will make them money
Solve user problem	Solve money problem
All about you and your solution	All about them and their problem

You need to stop any one-way sales education meetings, the ones that are all about you, and start developing sales strategies for conducting a sales education call that has mutual benefit (see Chapter 8: Educate the Customer Using Two-Way Learning). FB selling does work in an educational sale to a User Buyer. It's easier, also, since you do not have to find out what the value to the buyer is. In many cases, the User Buyer doesn't know or care about value.

However, use FBV statements to gain a competitive advantage. In addition, FBV selling helps to *ProActively* induce transfer of ownership, since you are working with the prospect to determine the real worth of the solution you are offering. FBV is hard to insert every time, but when you do use this tool, you and the prospect see things through the same lens and end up working together, since you both have WIIFM interests and are both interested in satisfying the customer's real problems.

Continue FB selling if you're always selling to the User Buyer. Sell FBV to the Business Buyer and you will shorten your sales cycle and increase your average sales price.

Evaluate your current sales presentations. Are they one-way, requiring that the prospect sit and listen to you (*"I know it's thirty-five slides but I got it down to fifteen, and I can get through them in a hurry."*)? These are sales presentation *disasters!* The problem is you may not think they are disasters and, perhaps, neither does your User Buyer. The Business Buyer, however, will always consider such presentations to be disasters.

The Split

The Split is a buyer-centric event—it happens on the buyer side and not the sales side, which is why most salespeople miss it. For ProActive sales-

Figure 2-1 Business/Technical Split: Overview

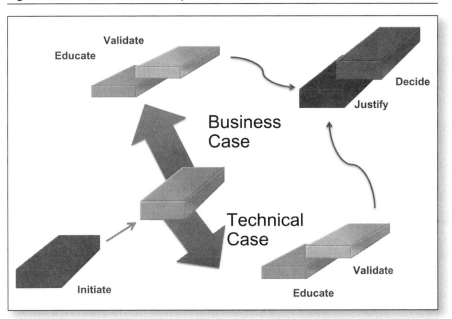

people to be aware of the split and sell to it, they must, again, think like a buyer.

Early in the purchasing process, the issues, challenges, concerns, and problems that buyers are encountering and trying to resolve split into two areas: the Technical Case and the Business Case (see Figure 2-1).

It's paying attention to the split between business and technical that will help you win the sale.

The Technical Case

The Technical Case is made for the kind of sale, heavily focused on features and benefits, that is geared to the User Buyer. User Buyers have been chartered to get something, do it within a budget, and somehow make it work and/or fix a problem. Since they are the ones who are going to have the responsibility of making the product/solution work, they need to know every detail, competitive advantage, packaging option, and price break they can get. After all, they are going to be "stuck" with you and your company's product/service, and they want it to work so they can look like heroes. Conversely, if they pick the wrong solution, they will cost the company money and will look incompetent.

Selling companies know this as well. They have their product marketing folks make sure the sales team is geared for these types of Technical Case/User Buyer sales. The tools available to the salesperson for this type of sale are many:

+ Company overview presentation
+ Product presentations
+ Testimonials on successful usage of product/service
+ White papers on the technology
+ Demonstrations of the product/service
+ Reference calls to other users
+ Plant visit to see the product/service in use or being built
+ Marketing collateral
+ Product fact sheets
+ Proposal generators
+ Proposal templates
+ Pricing models
+ Packaging schemes

And much, much more.

Business Case

The Business Case is for the kind of sale that focuses on two areas: problems and money. It's these two business issues that keep executives awake at night.

1. They have a problem they need to solve.
2. They need a better return on investment than they are getting currently

Let's look at each in turn.

Solving a Problem

The principal reason your prospects at a Business Case level will talk to you is because they have to do something they hate to do. They have to change something, and for the most part, people hate to change.

However, they are willing to change if they have a problem they need to solve, resolve, get off their desk, minimize, lessen, and implement—the kind of problems that consume their time. The buyers want to take some action.

Making More Money

One of the main drivers at this Business Case level is money, coming from one of two areas: Either what they are doing today is costing them too much money ("money" can include time, risk, soft dollars, hard dollars, and ROI, to name a few), or there is an opportunity to make more money by doing something different or better.

Remember the "customer's mission statement" in Chapter 1? This must become your Business Case Mantra:

CSP—Customers Solve Problems

If there is not an overriding business problem that the prospect is trying to solve and that your product or service can solve, the likelihood of getting a sale is greatly diminished. Why would a company invest in what you are selling if it didn't solve a problem or make them money?

> The reason cloud computing is so hot right now is not the technology (Technical Case/User Buyer). It's because of the Business Case: It costs a lot less, it's an operating expense not a capital investment in hardware/software, and it's faster and less cumbersome to grow with.

Here are some of the tools you can use at the Business Case level.

TOOL Cause/Effect^{Tool}

The Cause/Effect^{Tool} is a sales tool that responds to buyers splitting the sale between the Technical Case and the Business Case. The Effects part of this tool, geared to the User Buyer interested in the Technical Case, are *needs*. Each sale has a list of requirements or needs the buyer has identified for the product/service that is being bought. It's these *effects* that most salespeople love to sell to, since it's usually all about their products and services; in other words, the Feature/Benefit sale. "Effects" questions you ask the prospect here are:

- ◆ What are you looking for? What is the overriding need?
- ◆ What do you want it to do?
- ◆ When do you need it by?
- ◆ What is your budget?
- ◆ How do we stack up against the competition?
- ◆ We have a new model coming out in a few months. Want to see it?
- ◆ When would you like to see a demo?

Since salespeople have control over these questions, and can take action on these effects, they feel comfortable asking these questions and feel, when the buyer responds to them, that they are getting closer to a sale.

The Cause part of the tool represents the *motivation* behind the sale. This part of the tool is geared to Business Case Buyers. With this sale, you want to determine what is *causing* the company to take some action, do something different, or make a change to a current process. You need to find out what is *causing* the company to spend executive time and money on this issue, what is *driving the action*. The Action Driver questions you ask at this level are different than those you would ask at the Effects level, and include:

- ◆ What is the *cause* for leaving the current state and trying to achieve different results?
- ◆ What is the *urgency* to achieve the different results?
- ◆ What is the *impact, payback,* or *return* that is expected?
- ◆ What are the *consequences* of staying at the current state and not doing anything?
- ◆ What are the available *resources, options,* or *means* to achieve the results?

The Differences

The differences between the Technical Case Buyer and the Business Case Buyer are obvious (see Figure 2-2). The Technical Case/User Buyer wants to know all about what you have to offer. The Business Case Buyer couldn't care less what you are selling, as long as it solves a problem or makes them money. The split occurs early in the buy

Figure 2-2 Business/Technical Split: Cause and Effect

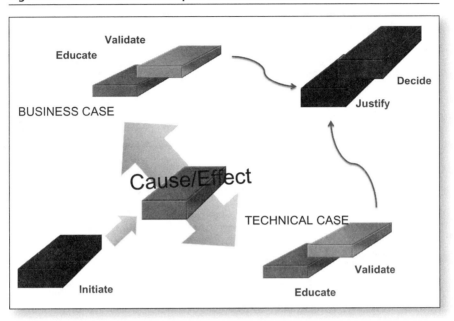

process. The more senior-level prospect identifies a problem or need to change for the organization, and then empowers the lower-level User Buyer to take action.

Instead of being ProActive, most salespeople honor the split much later in the sales process, thinking that all that is left for the salesperson to do when they get to the Business Case Buyer is "check in." Hah! Big mistake.

The Check-In

In Figure 2-3, you see a typical Buy/Sell process. Once a prospect has an Initial Interest, they move to the Educate step, at which point the deal splits into the two levels (A). Salespeople, wanting to talk about themselves and win the sale, go to the Technical Case (B). They proceed along the sales process until (C), the Justify step, which usually includes a proposal.

At this point, when it's time to ask for money, the salesperson knows they need to call high in the organization to "check in" with the person who has the financial authority.

Figure 2-3 Business/Technical Split: A Process View

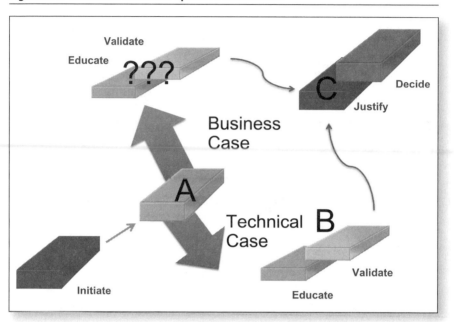

"Hello Ms. Wright, I'm David Salinger from XYZ Company. We've been talking to Daisy in the operations group about our product/service, and she really likes what we are offering. So if you have a moment, I'd like to bring you up to speed on what we do and how it is going to benefit Daisy and your company."

The salesperson then breaks into the slide show to give the decision makers an executive overview of what he's been talking to the User Buyer about, why his product/service is uniquely qualified, and a background of his company so the decision makers "feel good" about who they are doing business with.

The problem here is the Business Case Buyer *couldn't care less* what you are doing with the User Buyer. They have their own issues, and if you can't help them with their issues, why would they want to meet with you? If you think you can give the C-level buyers an update on what you have been doing with their User Buyer, remember: their User Buyer is already keeping them updated.

Success Patterns

When salespeople get a shot at calling high in the organization, they get nervous, and usually fall back on "success patterns." These are behaviors that have worked for them in the past. You probably have your own "success patterns": It could be making a particular presentation, bringing in a particular executive or technical product expert you've done well with on sales calls in the past, or even how you format final proposals. There are numerous success patterns in which salespeople firmly believe (probably somewhat more effective than wearing your lucky blue blazer, but not much). If they had success with them before, why try anything new?

Unfortunately, these success patterns are almost invariably geared for the User Buyer/Technical Case level and don't really work well at the Business Case level. The results are mixed, at best.

Get to the Business Case Buyer Early in the Game

To avoid getting to the Business Case level too late, ProActive salespeople treat this sale—at the Educate level, when the deal splits—as two sales: the Technical Case and the Business Case. In other words, they work *both* levels *early* in the process. They don't wait until they get to the formal proposal at the Justify stage to talk to the Business Case Buyer; and when they've reached the Business Case Buyer, they talk feature/benefits/value, not features/benefits.

While they'll ask product *effect* questions to the User Buyer, they'll ask business *cause* questions to the Business Case Buyer.

Here's how it might work:

In the world of sales training, there are usually two different buyers.

The Technical Case Buyer

The Technical/User Buyer would be the Head of Sales Training or a first-line sales manager. When asked what they want in a sales training effort, they usually respond with:

> *"I need to have the salespeople qualify better."*
> *"I want to have my salespeople call higher in the organization."*
> *"We need to improve our listening skills."*

"We need to sell value and solutions."

"Salespeople need to control the sales cycle better."

Business Case Buyer

The Business Case Buyer would be the Vice President of Sales or even the CEO. The Business Case Buyer wants want something totally different, for example:

1. Increase forecast accuracy by 15 percent.
2. Lower cost of sales by 5 percent."
3. Increase ASP (average sales price) by 10 percent."
4. Go broad and deep and penetrate current accounts by 100K/account."
5. Minimize sales turnover by 30 percent.
6. Lower customer churn rate by 5 percent.
7. Avoid multiple sales processes in the company because it usually leads to 20 percent longer selling time than necessary.

Here's a story that puts the Cause/Effect tool into perspective.

One of my salespeople, Tim, went on a sales call, meeting with the Sales and Marketing Vice-President for a company looking to do some sales training. After the meeting, Tim called me with what he believed was great news. The conversation went something like this:

"Skip, this is unbelievable. I told them about the tools we offer, why we can really help their salespeople get better, and what salespeople typically say about how they use our tools on a daily basis. They told me their overriding need is to have their salespeople call higher in the organization, and we agreed we can help them do that. Overall, it was a great call."

"Great, Tim, but I have a few questions. What was the business driver? What is causing them to invest in sales training?"

"Well, they said they want to call higher in the organization and sell solutions."

"Why do they want to do that?" I asked.

"Well, they want to increase their revenue, obviously," Tim proclaimed.

"By how much and by when?"

"How should I know? I'm sure it's by a lot or they wouldn't be talking to me."

Knowing this was not going to have a good ending, we agreed to meet the next day.

"Tim, let's go over the Action Driver questions. Do we have any firm answers here?"

"Not really, Skip. I was really excited when they told me they had heard of us and really liked what they heard about what we offer."

"OK, that's good Tim, but let's call the VP back and ask him some of these Action Driver questions."

Two days later, Tim came into my office.

"I cannot believe the VP had answers to my questions. Why didn't he say something during the first meeting?" Tim wondered. Then he continued:

"They need to grow revenue next year by 20 percent, and he felt without getting his sales team more comfortable with senior-level sales methods, he was going to fall about 50 percent short of that growth number. Additionally, he has lost a few of his key salespeople, and feels that with sales training, his sales retention rate will double. He feels the investment he is going to make in sales training will help solve these problems. He also said the consequence of doing nothing was unacceptable."

"Did he say what features of the sales training you went over in the meeting are most important to him?"

"I asked him. He really didn't remember. All he said was he is going to approve what the regional sales managers want to do, as long as the head of sales training agrees. He's just making the investment so he has a better shot at making his numbers."

"So what are you going to do next time you have a C-Level sales call?" I asked.

"Stick to the Action Driver questions. The way I see it, there is a business reason behind his decision to invest, and there is also a business reason on why he was willing to see me. I was so excited he granted me the meeting; I just wanted to tell him about how we are going to help him. I learned my lesson."

Tim learned that there are two parts of a sale that day. He uncovered:

1. The motivating factors, that is, the business issues that are *causing* the prospect to want to do something different than what they are doing today.

2. The effects or needs on which the User Buyer will base the decision to buy the sales training program they want to implement.

If none of these business drivers or motivating factors exist, or if you fail to discuss these with the Business Case Buyer, your chance of success has just dropped. Now you have to rely on need-satisfying FB selling and hope they can figure out value.

The choice is yours. Be ProActive and get to the Split early, in the Education step, and when you are there, use FB selling for the User Buyer and FBV for the Business Case Buyer. Ask *effect* questions to the User Buyer for their needs, and ask *cause* questions to find out the motivation of the Business Case Buyer. Once you have identified their motivation—always either to solve a problem or make money/lower costs—you can address it effectively. They have to change anyway, so why not with the help of *your* product/service? Pretty simple, right?

CHAPTER 3

The Language of Value

Speak the Right Language

You can prospect in person or over the phone, but the conversation is typically a dialog between interested or soon-to-be mutually interested parties, the seller and the buyer. The physical act of prospecting, dialing the phone or knocking on a door, is something anyone can do. The real issue, or better yet the question that needs to be addressed before you pick up that phone or start to knock on a door, is:

> "What do I say to the person when I start talking? I can dial the phone or go door to door. That's easy. When I get someone on the line or see them face-to-face, what do I say? How do I begin the conversation so they are interested in what I have to say?"

Many salespeople have a fear of prospecting. What they really fear is the frustration and hassle of rejection. Good salespeople know the first minute of prospecting is crucial, since rapport is built early and the conversation follows from that first minute. So why do salespeople avoid prospecting? What is this big fear of prospecting?

That First Minute of Prospecting Fear

"You know, my problem is not prospecting. I can do that. My problem is the first minute. If I can get their attention for a minute and then build rapport off of that, then I know I'll be okay. It's that first minute, or even the message I have to leave on voice mail to get someone to call me back . . . that's what I struggle with. Get me past that first minute of conversation, or give me a voice mail message that will get them to call me back, and then I am set."

It's easy to overcome this fear and become very powerful during the first minute of prospecting, as well as during your entire prospecting process. It all hinges on how effectively you communicate to the person you are talking to—and on *speaking the right language*. And we have a tool that will help you with that, the Three Languages™ (see Figure 3-1).

TOOL **Three Languages**™

There are three levels of buyers in every organization that you, as a salesperson, will deal with, and each level *has its own language*. Not only do companies speak three languages, but it is your job to speak the right language to the right person at the right time—and speak it well.

Figure 3-1 Three Languages™

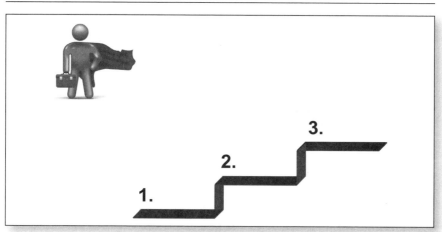

The First Level and Language

The first level is the person in the customer's organization you would typically call on all the time. Typical titles these Level 1 people would have include:

- Manager
- Manufacturing Manager
- Engineer
- Purchasing Agent
- Director
- IT Manager
- Office Manager
- Engineering Manager
- Buyer
- Marketing Manager
- Store Manager

First-level buyers are those at the managerial level. Managers speak the language of Feature/Function (see Figure 3-2).

"Does your solution come with training?"
"Does the system have the latest features on it?"
"Can I get expedited delivery?"

Figure 3-2 Three Languages™: Manager Level

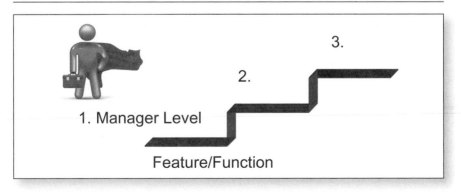

"How does this compare with last year's model?"
"Where can I see one working?"

Managers are very interested in the feature/function of the product/solution on its own merits. To sell to managers, salespeople must be able to have a discussion with them and be able to answer their questions. Salespeople therefore are always attending product and services training and reading a ton of company brochures and manuals every chance they get to make sure they don't have to say, "I don't know." Product and technical competence are at issue here, and salespeople want to be fully prepared, so they learn about the product or services they sell. This product/service training translates into:

- Features knowledge
- Feature/benefit statements
- Feature/advantage/benefit statements
- Competitive features
- Product-focused value propositions

Salespeople are given a host of information on these topics, so when they have a dialog with the managers who speak Feature/Function, they can say the right thing to the right people at the right time.

"Our product can do this 20 percent faster than the current product you are using, because our product has a special feature called . . ."
"Using this new feature on the GL-3000 will allow you to really make the system hum."
"By using our GLM, GSM, and GMAX modules, you will be able to manufacture those parts much faster than before."
"Our methodology and the way we deliver our service to you will allow for a much smoother integration."

The manager level is where most salespeople make their calls and spend most of their time, so it becomes obvious that salespeople need to become very fluent in this language. Company resources therefore are focused on this language since here is where salespeople demand the most from their company. This includes the marketing department as well as other support organizations.

The Second Level and Language

Companies also speak a second-level language, however. This is the language of most vice presidents (see Figure 3-3). Vice presidents say something like:

> "Thanks for coming . . . really, thanks for coming. You are 20 percent faster than xyz . . . I didn't know that . . . really . . . and you are 30 percent smaller than previous models . . . really? . . . I didn't know that . . . and you are x.556.75z compatible . . . really? . . . I didn't know that . . . wow . . . thanks for coming . . . really . . . thanks for that information . . . really, thanks . . . BUT . . . If you can't make me money or save me money, why am I talking with you?"

For all vice presidents, there are only two reasons to do anything in business, and those are to increase revenue or decrease cost. How are you going to increase their revenue or decrease their cost?

A vice president is chartered to make corporate goals. Corporate goals are always stated in fiscal terms: earnings, earnings before insurance and taxes (EBIT), net present value of investments (NPV), revenue per employee, compound annual growth rate (CAGR), as well as a host of other fiduciary measurements. A vice president is chartered with the health of the business, and along with that mandate is the responsibility that all major decisions that affect their organization be fiscally sound ones.

You need to know what vice presidents are really interested in as it relates to what you are selling. What are their hot buttons? What is really

Figure 3-3 Three Language^{Tool}: Vice President Level

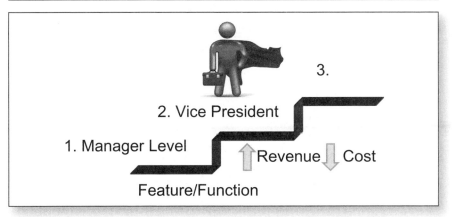

important to them? What are they willing to take action on? The answer is *value* and the *value proposition*. And, as you remember the Buyer's Value Proposition from Chapter 1, what's important to them is *their* value proposition, not yours.

Value proposition from the seller's point of view:

- ♦ We have offices in twenty-two locations around the world.
- ♦ It took us four years to develop this product.
- ♦ We hire only the smartest people.
- ♦ We integrate with eighty-five different systems.
- ♦ We have had twenty-two quarters of positive earnings.
- ♦ Our product is 20 percent better than its closest competitor.
- ♦ Our corporation is now leading the charge for this industry.

Great, really great, but the vice president wants to know, "What is in it for me?" Too many salespeople deliver the value proposition of their company and assume that the customer can translate what it will mean to their organization—and to their organization's bottom line. In every conversation you have, whether in business or in your personal life, whenever you let someone interpret the meaning of what you have said, you have a possibility of miscommunication. A ProActive salesperson understands that the vice president wants to know WIIFM. Vice presidents want to know what the value is for *them* in your solution.

The Third Level and Language

The third-level language that companies speak is reserved for senior management: presidents, senior vice presidents, executive vice presidents, CFOs, CEOs, CIOs, and so on (see Figure 3-4). At the top of the list of things they care about are market share and market size. That's about it. How big is the market, how big can it get, and how much share of this market can the company get? (How much share can I, the CEO, have, maintain, preserve, take, cover, and develop as well?)

While talking to people at this level, you need to focus on market share and market size. It is their lifeblood, their focus, and their ultimate measure. How much pie is there and how much of that pie can I get? This is what third-level managers talk about.

Figure 3-4 Three Languages™: Senior Management Level

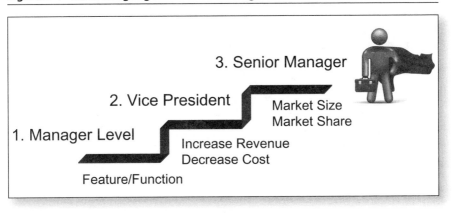

The Three Languages in a Business Process

A real-life business process will help illustrate the concept of the three languages. Level 3 managers need to go to their bosses (stakeholders, shareholders, owners, board of directors, and so on) every year and, in most cases, every quarter to report on the state of the business as well as current and future plans. Level 3 managers say to their bosses something like this:

> "The market is growing 14 percent CAGR over the next three years. If you adopt and approve my plans, we will profitably grow the business 3 percent over the next three years."

Unusual circumstances aside, if a president went to his board and made this statement, how long do you think he would be able to keep his job? Not very long, that's for sure. What the president needs to say is:

> "The market is growing 14 percent CAGR over the next three years. If you adopt and approve my plans, we will profitably grow the business 19 percent over the next three years and take significant share away from our competitors."

This is a much better picture, and if this happens, and the board/shareholders/stakeholders approve these plans, the president will be funded for another year.

Now that the president has been funded, he goes to his Level 2 managers and gives them budgets for the fiscal year and then tells them to manage the budgets so they come in under budget but do not go over. They need to deliver 10 percent more top line (revenue) while holding bottom line (costs) to budget. These are common requests Level 3 managers make to Level 2 managers.

Now that Level 2 managers have budgets, they formulate, reexamine, plot, manipulate, devise, and assign these budgets to different departments in their organization. How are budgets allocated? Which Level 1 manager, who works for the Level 2 manager, has the best ideas that are going to help the Level 2 manager meet her budget? The department or the people who have the best ideas to help the vice president make her business goals (budget) will get more than their fair share of the limited resource (money) for the year.

It all plays out from there. The great ideas get more budget money, they help the Level 2 manager make her budget, and since they were great ideas, they did better than budget, and therefore helped the Level 3 manager increase market share. However, what level of language is the most important level to speak? What language is the most productive for ProActive salespeople to master so they can win more deals and increase their sales? The answer is clear: Salespeople must learn to speak the language of the Level 2 manager most fluently, that is the Language of Value—value for the customer.

Why the ProActive Salesperson Must Become Multilingual

Before you get into the Language of Value, the three languages need to be anchored, since the languages are a concept that most salespeople are aware of, but just do not know what to do with.

There is a huge push in most sales organizations nowadays to call higher in the organization. Call at the top, at the senior management level. Sell to VITO (very important top officer).

Calling high by itself is not the trick. Anybody can call high. The trick is knowing what to say when you call high in an organization. What do you say to a senior-level executive that will let you be seen as a value-add and not just as a salesperson who is trying to peddle something?

One of the great fears of every salesperson is that, after meeting with a senior executive, the senior executive thinks the salesperson adds little value to them, and will end up passing the person down in their organization to a lower level. He or she will then have to jump through hoops to get back up to the senior level again.

What can you say to add value in these senior management sales calls? First, speak the right language.

Take the three levels of language we just discussed and identify each as a different actual language. For the Level 1 language, the manager level, assign "Spanish," for Level 2, the vice president level, "Russian," and for the senior manager level, Level 3, "Greek." You now have three languages, Spanish, Russian, and Greek.

Imagine you are prospecting at a higher level in a company, at a vice president level, also now called a Russian. You have one hour or less to impress and create an interest in what you are selling. You have your usual presentation material, your slides, and a projector. You have practiced your speech, your presentation starts, and you are doing great. As a matter of fact, you are quite pleased on how you are really getting into your speech. Having delivered this speech hundreds of times before, you are really good at it.

About fifteen minutes into the presentation, however, the vice president interrupts.

"Excuse me, but this presentation is in Spanish. I don't speak Spanish very well. Why don't you give this presentation to John and Mary who work for me, since they speak Spanish much more fluently than I do?"

This is not what he actually says, but it is what he means.

You are still feeling okay, since the vice president has told you to call John and Mary and you can reference the vice president to get the meeting. You actually can hear yourself making the phone call.

"Hi Mary, this is Chris Ross, and Mr. Hitchcock, your vice president, told me to call you."

How much more powerful a reference call can you get? You're thinking you'll get an immediate call back from John and Mary and a sure appointment. You're feeling good about being passed down. What Mr. Hitchcock, the vice president, didn't finish telling you during the call you had with him was what else he was thinking. You were too excited getting his reference to call John and Mary to ask.

"By the way, Chris, I don't speak Spanish anymore, which is the language your presentation is in. I am sure all these features and functions of what your product does are important to the people who speak Spanish who work for me, so please spend your time with my Spaniards, and they will tell me if what you have is important."

Mr. Hitchcock's thoughts continue:

"Quite frankly, Chris, I used to speak Spanish, but then I got promoted, and now I speak Russian. I'm also very busy trying to learn Greek. Any chance you can help me with that?"

This was a golden opportunity to offer the vice president something he is interested in. You've missed your opportunity, however, because you were too busy speaking Spanish to notice.

You are speaking the wrong language to the wrong person. You have no Spanish-to-Russian dictionary with you on this sales call, and you're out of luck. You prepared the call in Spanish and delivered it in Spanish. You hang out with Spanish buyers all the time, and you speak very good Spanish. Great, but it doesn't work with Russians. Speak the right language. Speak Spanish to a Spaniard, Russian to a Russian, and Greek to a Greek.

The Five Ways of Creating Value

So now that you know how to speak different languages, when you do speak to the Business Case, the "Russian," what do you say? You say nothing. You ask ValueStar questions in the Language of Value.

When you are talking to Russian as well as to Greek buyers, the Language of Value is the only language they know. It is imperative that you learn the Language of Value because speaking any other language to a Russian or Greek buyer is ineffective and a waste of your time (a valuable company resource). There are five ways of creating value, as follows:

- ◆ Return on Investment (ROI)
- ◆ Time
- ◆ Risk
- ◆ Leverage
- ◆ Brand

That's it. Value can be related in a sales environment through these five value points. It is called the ValueStar^{Tool}.

TOOL	The ValueStar^{Tool}

How do these points create value? How can a salesperson use value to sell to the upper levels of an organization? The points on the ValueStar (see Figure 3-5) will show you the way.

Create the Value: More than ROI

Return on Investment (ROI) is the measure organizations have used for years. It's the common vocabulary companies use to quantify what is important to them. Companies are always trying to increase revenue and decrease cost to maintain and increase their viability. It's their sole reason for being. Businesses want to grow profitably, and to do this, they must get a return on all the investments they make.

What do you sell? What do you really sell? When we ask salespeople this question, we usually get answers like:

♦ Solutions
♦ Services

Figure 3-5 ValueStar^{Tool}

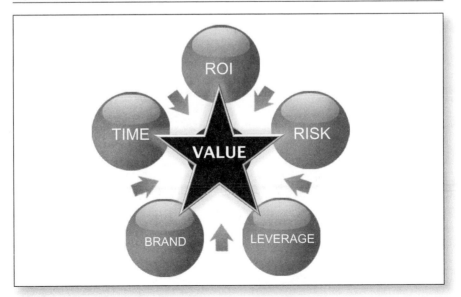

- Features and benefits
- Advantages
- A better way of doing something
- Value
- A total package
- Competitive advantages

To sell value, you must know there is only one thing you really sell: You sell money!

When involved in a purchasing decision, senior-level people care only about the return they are getting on their investment. That is it. It is all about money. Most Russians and Greeks are greedy. They want even more than just the amount of money they are "giving" you. They want more than their original investment back. They want two to three times the money they are giving you so they can invest that money into other ideas, so they can make even more money. It sounds simple, and it is, and it's based on the premise that you sell money.

One of our clients sells an annual service. It's a subscription-based service for which they charge their customers anywhere from $10,000 to $1,000,000+ per year. The vice president of sales told us once that he had a revelation one day. Here he was trying to sell his company's services and renew subscriptions every year. He thought he was actually selling a service. *"If the client paid us $200,000 per year, and we gave them $200,000 worth of our services, I thought everyone was happy."* With this thought, the vice president thought he was giving a fair service for a fair price.

"But then I realized that to senior people in the client organization I was just an investment they were making. Seems that they looked at our services differently from the way the users of our services look at us. Users of our services liked and appreciated what we did, our customer service, our methodology, the way we delivered information, and the way we improved on ways of doing things. Senior managers, however, have a different viewpoint. They view us as an investment, and they are interested in only one thing: How are they going to get their money back? What is the return on investment they are making? Oh, I'm sure they like us and think that our stuff is neat and cool, but all they care about is their investment. As a matter of fact, now that I know that I sell money, I can see that most of my customers actually want a return of two or three times on their investment."

Chris was lucky. He got to speak with the vice president, Mr. Hitchcock, a second time a few weeks later. They had a very different conversation. He told me:

> "I went back and changed my entire PowerPoint presentation. I looked at what I had, and I saw I wasn't speaking money. I was speaking Spanish. I now realized I must carry a Russian and Greek message when I call on senior managers. Now, when a salesperson goes on a sales call and needs someone to speak at a high level, they bring me. I am seen as a value-add on senior sales calls, and it's only because I speak money and ROI. I speak Russian."

ROI is the language the senior management team uses to talk about all investments the company is making, including the purchase of your goods/services. But ROI is a language salespeople do not feel comfortable discussing, since they really believe it is none of their business. Here are some of the things you might hear them say:

> *"I just tell them what they are buying. Soft dollars or hard dollars? I have no idea. It's up to them to figure out if they can justify it or not."*
>
> *"Can the prospect afford our solution? We're waiting to hear from them on this very issue right now. Personally, I have no idea what they are using to quantify the decision in financial terms, but I sure hope they can afford us.*
>
> *"ROI? It's not on one of my slides. I know our product and how the customer is supposed to use it. My bottom line is that I'll cut them a deal they will just find too hard to pass up."*

The salesperson who refuses to learn and discuss ROI will be the one who tries to sell on Feature/Function. This works for a Spaniard, but Russians have a different agenda.

Two Important Rules Regarding ROI

Rule #1: Russians live in a quantified world. *A ton, a bunch, a lot, huge,* and *vast* are great words, but have no meaning since they are not quantified. For ROI to have any value, the Russian must commit to a quantified number.

> *"That's worth $500,000 to me this year."*
>
> *"I can get a 3X return on this investment."*

"I can see an increase of 3 percent of my revenue for this expenditure. It's worth it."

"The only other option is twice as expensive and offers no other financial benefits. This is the right thing to do."

Rule #2: ROI figures have to come from the Russian. You cannot just present an Excel spreadsheet or a "best practices" white paper to them. These are obviously great tools for a Spaniard to take to a Russian, but not for a Russian sales call.

Senior managers can make numbers look almost any way they want them to look. ROI is the most used, but probably one of the least firm value points on the ValueStar. You have to know ROI, talk ROI, and work with ROI, but be ready to play with all the numbers. You have to challenge assumptions and get to the real meat of the ROI analysis. Bottom line, the ROI has to come from their lips, not yours. You cannot tell Russians what you are worth. You have to ask them, and they will tell you. They do it all the time. They are working on their solution, and they can figure out what piece of their solution you are worth to them. Ask them. If they can't tell you:

1.   There is no current executive solution they can use you for at this time. (In this case, disqualify the prospect—for now.)
2.   You are talking to the wrong person. (Is he really a Russian? Can you find the right person?)

Time: The Value Leverage

Time is the second point in the ValueStar, and with it comes a great deal of leverage. Time has many dimensions to it, and salespeople need to look past their single point of reference for time.

We talk about time constantly, all kinds of "time":

Talking About Time

Uptime	Just in time	Phasing out over time
Overtime	Right timing	In time
Down time	Time in market	Timing the launch
Timing of the market	Time to market	of a product

Anyone will pay for time, including you. You will pay more to drive on a toll road and get somewhere quicker than taking the back streets to your destination. That would take too much time. People will pay more to take a direct flight than one with a stopover. Customers will pay to be faster, quicker, and more rapid than they have been before.

Find out what's important to your customer from a time perspective. You'll find there are multiple time elements in most decisions. One person has certain time issues, and another person within the buying organization has other time issues that are very different from those of the first person. Companies have many time constraints, deadlines, and time-to-market issues. Your job as a ProActive salesperson is to find out as much as you can about the time issue your prospect has.

You cannot cheat time. Customers have only 24 hours in a day, 7 days in a week, 52 weeks in a year. There is no getting around it. Since it is a scarce and valuable resource, prospects value it highly. Find out what is important to them. It could be:

1. Getting a new product to market before a deadline, competitive offering, or compelling event such as a trade show or stockholders' meeting.
2. Getting new pricing or packaging out.
3. Doing something in less time.
4. Timing issues due to customer relationships.

The time list can go on and on. You want to have multiple bullets for the proverbial value gun, so make sure you have multiple time value issues. The more you have, the harder it is for the buyer to say no. Make it worth their time.

TOOL   TimeZones^Tool

The new TimeZones^Tool (see Figure 3-6) will help you prioritize your efforts to address the timing issues that are most important to the prospect or buyer. This tool highlights the three time zones on which buyers will be focused: the past, the present, and the future. This is a particularly useful tool for talking to a Russian.

Prospects who are focused on the _past_ will take action on something that is past-based, or "restorative." That is, they will spend energy and resources to restore things back to how they were. Just as you will spend

Figure 3-6 TimeZones^{Tool}

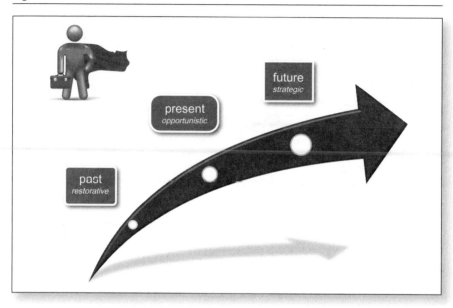

$400 for a tune-up to get your car running the way it did when you first bought it, a corporate prospect will:

♦ Invest in a new website that will attract as much as the old one did without all the "new" features.

♦ Do whatever it takes to get their revenue steams back to where they were before they reorganized incorrectly.

♦ Spend money to get its sales force as productive as it implemented that dreadful CRM system.

Prospects who are focused on the *present* will also make an investment for a present opportunity, what we can call an "opportunistic" decision. For example:

♦ There's a merger happening and we can take advantage of it right now.

♦ Our top competitor just went out of business.

♦ It's the start of the fourth quarter. Time to start selling.

There is always a present opportunity of which companies can take advantage.

Prospects who are focused on the *future* would make company-based "strategic" decisions. Strategic decisions are the main focus of executives. For example:

- We need to make this investment for next year's growth.
- I'm planning right now for the second half of the year.
- If we invest in this product now, it will pay dividends within eighteen months.

Russians spend most of their time making decisions that are focused on the past or the future. Spaniards, the User Buyers, think more about the present, because they are given a task to do and a time frame in which to achieve it. *"I have to solve this problem that my boss has given me,"* is how User Buyers think.

So given these three time elements, there is a huge difference between the following three questions:

1. "Mr. Smith, what are some of the time-sensitive issues you had to face in the first part of the year you really don't want to have to face again in the second half?"
2. "Mr. Smith, what is your most time-sensitive decision today?"
3. "Mr. Smith, from a timing perspective, what are the most critical decisions you are looking at over the next few months?"

As you can imagine, the Russians love questions 1 and 3, but have no context for question 2. They are trying to avoid the mistakes of the last six months, and make sure the next six months are smooth sailing. If a salesperson calls on them and asks a "present" question—*"So Mr. Smith, what is the biggest challenge you face today?"*—they wouldn't know what to answer.

Think of the past and the future as digital videos, because there is motion in your question, either past or future. Present questions do not have a time element to them, so call them digital photo questions. Figure 3-7 illustrates this concept.

To use the ValueStar tool effectively, your questions must be in the right TimeZone. They must be digital video questions. Make sure you "time travel" to the past and the future when you are posing ValueStar questions to a Russian.

Figure 3-7 TimeZones: Static or Dynamic?

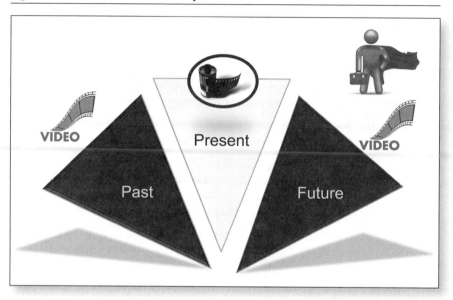

Risk: What It Is ALL About

Here lies the key to the kingdom. Value can mean different things to different people, and the objective and subjective nature of the ROI and Time points on the ValueStar can be debated. Will this new product/service *really* save that much time? How do they know they will *actually* get that kind of ROI? What if the schedule slips (and it always does)? Subjectivity and qualitative factors always start creeping into Russians' decision making, and the question becomes *"What is the risk?"* If you are looking for the key value point on the ValueStar that rises above them all, the bread and butter play, then look no further. You must talk, understand, and assist Russians in addressing and helping to mitigate their risks.

Risk is the key value factor that keeps senior executives up at night. Decisions at the lower level of the organization are quite binary—black and white, yes/no, now/later, up/down, or in/out. Decisions at the higher levels of companies are never that simple, which is why they need the involvement of a senior executive in the first place. Senior management decisions are much more complex and take into account so many other factors that they are fraught with risk. Risk is what makes senior executives turn their heads and take notice. They ask themselves the following questions:

"Was there something we forgot? Is there a market out there that someone forgot about, and therefore our current decisions are riskier?"

"Was everyone who needed to be involved, involved? Is there a potential for a communication breakdown that will grind this organization to a screeching halt?"

"Are we making the wisest choices with the limited resources we have?"

Senior managers want and need to talk about risk. Salespeople come in and talk to them, or at them, all the time. These salespeople ask questions, but not the right ones. They ask:

"What would your role be if your company wants to implement our solution?"

"Are you the final authority for deciding on this implementation?"

"I wanted our senior manager to meet with you. Is this okay?"

"We have been working with some of your people, and we just want to make sure we get your input."

"How do you see our relationship going forward?"

Are these the types of questions that keep Russians and Greeks awake at night? Not so much. Risk is what matters to them. They need to make many decisions daily, and none of them have a 100 percent confidence factor.

These are the kinds of questions you can profitably ask a Russian:

"What do you see as the biggest risk in a decision like this to you and your company in the next three to six months?"

"What have you thought about regarding this implementation and where you can minimize your risk?"

"How can we, working together, increase the probability of a successful outcome?"

"What do you see as the major risk factor with this project as you look to the next two to three quarters?"

"What are the risks you face in the next six months regarding this solution?"

Senior executives are eager to talk to you about risk. It is what they face daily, yet no salesperson wants to discuss it with them. Salespeople come into the office and try to sell something, usually speaking Spanish and spewing out a Feature/Function presentation.

Russians and Greeks care about value, and they really care about the risks their decisions are going to have on the organization. They ask:

> *"What will be the start-up risks associated with launching this new product now instead of next quarter?"*
>
> *"If I shut down capacity at this factory for a month to add this new piece of equipment, what are the start-up risks associated with that?"*
>
> *"What will the risks be to all of my departments if I add this new process into the organization?"*

Senior managers make decisions all they time. That's why they are senior managers. For every decision they make, every investment they have to make, for every act they have to justify, they have to weigh the risks. Make a Russian's decision safer, or less risky, and you will have their attention.

Leverage: Building Value Across Projects

Leverage is on the ValueStar to remind you that senior executives build value across projects, not just on one project. The goal here is for you to make sure the executives in your prospective company see you affecting multiple projects, not just one.

One way to think about leveraging value across projects is in terms of a train station (see Figure 3-8). The conductor of Train 1 may have brought you in, but now you get to have some time with the "station manager" (Russian). Your goal would not only be to confirm that you can help solve problems on Train 1, but also to ask about other trains that may have caused problems for the Station Manager over the last six months (past), or trains that may have trouble making their scheduled

Figure 3-8 Trains in the Train Station

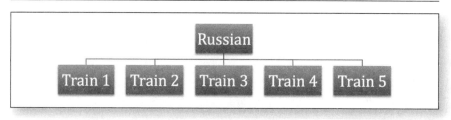

departure (future). Your goal is to find an opportunity to leverage your company solutions across multiple trains.

It's really scary for salespeople to go to a Russian meeting armed with nothing but questions. If they don't have their slide show, printed materials, customer success stories, samples, or at least a leave-behind, they feel naked and ask,

> "Why would this senior manager take time to come down from on high and speak with me? I better be prepared!"

Be prepared with questions that will help you uncover more trains. You can create leverage with your access to power by asking about multiple trains. Russians need answers to their train issues, problems, challenges, tasks, and concerns. They have to get the trains out of the station, and they would rather talk about their trains than your products and services any day of the week. Create value leverage by asking about their trains. (See Chapter 8 to learn about our Finding Trains^Tool.)

Brand: The Wrapping Paper and Bow

The final point on the ValueStar is Brand or Image. Brand also includes quality, since quality is usually in the eye of the beholder, and is more perception than reality.

Brand or Image takes shape in the form of:

- The product
- The company
- The customers you have
- The salesperson and sales manager
- The company history
- The marketing literature
- The customer support you offer
- The website you maintain
- The last sale you made
- The contract you ask the customer to sign
- The proposal you gave the customer
- The letters and e-mail you use to correspond with the customer
- The logo of your company

Brand is where emotions and perceptions come into play, and you need to find out what is really important to each buyer in the prospect's organization. Brand plays to perceptions. It can be as simple as, *"I always buy a Sony, since I know the quality will be high,"* to *"I trust Lisa and her company. Her professionalism has been demonstrated throughout this evaluation."*

In the first example, the Brand is based on reputation and past history, but it still is a personal, emotional rationalization. In the second example, the Brand is based on the actions of the salesperson and how she represents her company. Remember that in both examples, the prospect is transferring this idea of Brand to their own decision-making process. It's as if the prospect is saying to herself:

> *"Since I am buying from Lisa* (or from *Sony), I am like them. I have a perception that I want to be associated with, and Lisa* (or *Sony) represents the idea of Brand that I want other people to judge me by."*

Emotional ownership transfers with Brand, and it can be personal or organizational. It's important to discuss with your customers what your product/service will do for their Brand. If you can improve their competitiveness, make them look better by associating with you, or lessen the risk of their customers who buy their products, you create leverage and create value. Think from your customers' perspective as well as your own.

The ValueStar is a unique way of defining how salespeople should arm themselves ProActively and sell what the buyer is asking for, not what the seller wants to sell them.

ValueStar Defined

The ValueStar is your key to being multilingual in a prospect's organization. If you spend half the time learning the key areas of the ValueStar that you spend learning product knowledge and Feature/Function knowledge, imagine how fluently you could sell to value.

Finally, you may find yourself in a meeting at which multiple languages are being spoken at the same time. You may have a few Spaniards and a Russian in a meeting, and sometimes even a Greek shows up. (By the way, Greeks love speaking Russian; it gets them back in the business where they love to play.) The question most salespeople have at this juncture is, *"What language do I speak in the meeting?"*

The answer is always to speak up; speak to the higher level. When a Spaniard is in a meeting with a Russian, you need to speak Russian.

Managers know they must speak the language of their bosses to get promoted. Good managers know that if they want to get their project approved or to even be considered for a promotion, they need to become multilingual and learn Russian. How many times have you been in a meeting with a Spaniard and a Russian, and the Spaniard only wants to speak in Spanish, and the Russian gets annoyed since she is left on her own to translate between Spanish and Russian? Worse, there are times where there are multiple Spaniards in the room, and they want to dominate the conversation and not even let you get a word in with the Russian. (I call this a Spanish Inquisition. The Spaniards dominate the conversation by asking a host of Feature/Function questions, and you are forced to speak in Spanish during the entire presentation.)

It is the wise Spaniard who can translate Spanish into Russian for the vice president, since the vice president will view that Spaniard as someone who is credible and thinks the right way. The Russian then looks differently at this particular manager, since the Russian believes this Spaniard has the ability to think like a Russian and see things from a Russian's perspective. The Spaniard who can express what he wants or what the need truly is *in Russian* gets what he wants—and is also considered promotable.

When in doubt, speak up. Speak the right language to the right person, and you will communicate your product/service value proposition much more powerfully than ever before.

Armed with the knowledge of who you should call on and what you should say, you are now ready for your first sales call. It is time actually to prospect.

CHAPTER 4

Initiate

BUYERS BEGIN THEIR BUYING PROCESS with an Initial Interest, which means the salesperson—you—should begin by generating initial interest with a selling phase called "Initiate."

For you to be ProActive, you must master the early part of the sales process, which is much more important than the ending or closing part. For now, forget learning all those closing techniques, and focus on where you can really make a difference. The better you are in setting up the sale correctly, the better qualified and cleaner the deal will be. Therefore, generating initial interest is a very important step in every sale. The overall goal of this phase is to:

♦ Introduce yourself, your company, and your product/service to the prospect.

♦ Interest the prospect in your product/service.

♦ Determine whether there is a reason to continue the process.

That's it. This part of Initiate is very simple, with no pressure or prospecting stress. Too many salespeople believe the goal of Initiate, or prospecting, is to get an order or an appointment. Why would you want to put that much pressure on yourself? The goal of Initiate is simple:

1. Here's who I am and who my company is.
2. Here's what we do and how it could benefit what you do.
3. Should we continue on through a Buy/Sell process?

If you have a receptive prospect and think the prospect wants to continue on as well, then you should go for it. If either of you chooses not to continue on (disqualify), for whatever reason, then you should try again later with this prospect or move on to another one. It must be a mutual decision. You are now probably asking yourself:

"How can this be a mutual decision? What if they don't return my phone calls or my e-mails? What if they don't get back to me? How can I choose to continue on if they don't get back to me?"

All these questions will be answered later in this chapter. The current discussion is about the goal of Initiate, and what the overall structure is.

Remember that the goal in Initiate is not to "get an order" or "get a commitment" or "get an appointment." If you shoot for these goals, you will be disappointed. They are too hard, your chance of success is minimal, and, quite frankly, they are very one-dimensional. Instead, your goal should be to focus on the three goals of this stage: introduce yourself, introduce what you do, and determine whether to proceed.

Both the salesperson and the prospect need to determine whether to move forward. It must be a win-win since people have an aversion to being sold at or to. This is easy to say, but somewhat difficult to pull off in practice.

Goals of Initiate

Goal 1: Introduce Yourself

Your first goal is to introduce yourself and your company in a concise, clear, and professional manner. If you have a unique or difficult name to pronounce, be extra careful to enunciate it so the prospect does not have to guess at who you are, and go S . . . L . . . O . . . W. Give the listener time to absorb and think.

Goal 2: Introduce Your Product/Service

This is where you patiently discuss what is currently important to the prospect, and based on previous knowledge gathered through homework or information gathered during this call, try to introduce in an effective way what you have to offer the client. This may sound simple, but the approach here is crucial. Too many buyers are literally being attacked by salespeople with their message.

> *"Call me back today to discuss what we are all about . . ."*
> *"I'm sure you would be interested in what we have to offer . . ."*
> *"Please call me back if what I have said about what we do is of interest to you . . ."*
> *"You need what we have . . ."*
> *"Once you understand our value proposition . . ."*

These are probably the most common approaches, and none of them are very effective. The goal here is to introduce successfully what you do, so the buyer understands and relates your product or service to their issues and concerns.

Goal 3: Should We Continue on Through a Buy/Sell Process?

Now that you have achieved the first two goals of generating interest, both you and the prospect need to decide whether you should continue at this time. By definition then, this is a mutual Buy/Sell process. If either the buyer or the salesperson thinks that further action at this time would not be a good idea, then the process should be called off and possibly revisited at a later time. If both decide to continue on, then you should go to the next phase in the process, which is Educate.

Here are some caveats regarding the goals of Initiate:

♦ Buyers may want to get together but need time to mull it over, so they stall. The reason for most stalls is that you are proposing changing what they do, or what they have scheduled already, and most people are uncomfortable with change.

They then propose another time and date for a meeting, say three months out. Or they say it is interesting, and tell you to call back later.

♦ They might tell you to go and talk to someone else first and then get back to them.

♦ They may even try to delay or come up with a "hidden objection" as to why this is not a good time right now.

♦ They may believe they already have a solution in place that does what you do. A salesperson is rarely going to hear on the phone, *"Yes, I am very interested in what you have to say, I'll clear my calendar. What would be a good time for you?"*

It's time for a reality check!

Buyers may be tentative and may have some interest, but do not want to be sold to. They do not want to change what they are doing, the way they are currently thinking, or the ideas they currently hold dear. So you need to adjust your style and approach to help them through this change, without adjusting the overall goals. You will learn how to help the prospect with these fears later on with some ProActive sales tools.

Once both parties understand that either one can call off this process at any time, it becomes easier to accomplish the objectives of Initiate. Neither of you has to feel pressured. It's a mutual decision.

Finally, the actual work involved in prospecting is never easy, nor is it a tremendous amount of fun. If you are looking for a book or a sales method that will make prospecting a great deal easier, you will not find it here. What this book does show you is how to make your prospecting more *effective*—far more effective than it has ever been before.

In the Initiate phase you need to:

♦ Determine the prospect's needs.

♦ Interest the prospect in your offering.

♦ Use the Summarize, Bridge, and Pull^{Tool} (see Chapter 5) to move to the next stage, Educate.

To accomplish these and prospect successfully, you need to:

1. Do your homework—the work required before you make any sales contact with a prospect.

2. Make the prospecting call itself—the actual contact you make with a prospect.

Homework Before the Sale

The first part of Initiate (the buyer's "Initial Interest") is homework. Get familiar with the account and the industry before you start selling into it.

Homework is critical in any profession. Indy car drivers check out their race cars before the race, musicians tune their instruments before the concert, and a surgeon checks over the operating room instruments before the operation. The amount and type of homework you accomplish before the sales call is a key to success.

The amount of homework should vary based on the size of the opportunity and the overall importance to the company. You will do more homework on a large potential account than you will for a very small opportunity. A company with annual sales of $250,000,000 would probably get more attention from you than an account with $250,000 in annual revenue.

For you, homework is the amount of work needed to get enough information on the account to discuss intelligently the business issues that are important to the customer. It may take five minutes or five hours for any given account. It can be as easy as checking out a website or as involved as engaging in a deep financial investigation. Simple questions that you might want answered include:

1. What is the prospect's annual revenue?
2. What is the prospect's current market share and market size?
3. What are the projections for revenue and market share and market size for the next twelve months?
4. What are the prospect's top two competitive advantages and how do you contribute in making them more competitive?
5. What is the mission of the company and what are the top three items on its corporate agenda?

Make sure you do whatever homework is required or recommended before every prospecting call—even if it's just a matter of looking at the annual report to see if one of the executives have worked for a customer of yours, or conducting a LinkedIn search to know if your prospect knows someone you may know. It's always better to start a prospecting conversation off on some common ground, rather than, *"So, what do you know about my company?"*

Your homework is done, and you are ready to make some prospecting calls. You know what company to call on, who to call on, what is important to them, and what you are going to say.

Initial Sales Calls: Overcoming the Fear of Prospecting

Salespeople will do so many things, go through so many hoops, and go to absolutely amazing lengths when they are involved in a sale, and then delight in the stories afterwards of what they had to go through to get a sale. Selling is fun. Getting a sale is fun. You love selling.

Change the subject to *prospecting*, however, and you get an entirely different narrative. The very word "prospecting" is emotionally charged. Prospecting is scary, frustrating, tedious, . . . it's something different for each of us, but usually, something negative. Selling is fun, but most salespeople would rather just sell and take the word "prospecting" out of their vocabulary completely. Some salespeople claim to love to prospect; most dislike it—and dislike is a mild word for how they really feel.

> *"Prospecting is something I have to do to get the sale going. I hate it, and I am not good at it."*
>
> *"Prospecting is tough. It's tough to take all those 'no thank you' calls and even tougher to take someone not even bothering to call you back. It makes you feel so insignificant, so second class."*
>
> *"If I can just get past the first minute or so of a prospecting call, then I'm fine. It's that first minute of building rapport and creating an interest that I just can't get past."*

With attitudes like these, it is easy to see why salespeople would rather avoid the whole prospecting arena. Prospecting is never easy, but you first need to put the entire issue of prospecting into place. The law of prospecting is simple, yet controversial.

THE LAW OF PROSPECTING

If you want to have customers in the pipeline, you have to prospect. If you want good prospects in your pipeline, you have to do it yourself.

Our friends at CSO Insights annually survey thousands of sales managers and salespeople. The results are consistent. Roughly 50 percent of all good prospects come from the direct work of an individual salesperson. Again, you have to do it yourself.

Salespeople and organizations will expend a huge amount of energy and resources to get prospects. They divide their attention among lead generation, lead generation activities, qualified leads, initial sales discussions, initial contacts, trade show leads, and reference leads. The list could keep going. Here are some basic facts regarding prospecting.

◆ If you want good prospects, you are going to have to hunt for them yourself, period.

◆ Most salespeople would rather do *anything* other than prospect . . . and they will come up with every justifiable reason in the book why today is not the right day to prospect—the stars are not aligned right, the marketing material is inadequate, or they are just not yet ready to do a good job at it.

◆ Activities to gather key names and opportunities are good homework and can be done by others. Inbound sales qualification can be done by an inside sales team. The actual contact to the customer, however, especially at the senior level, should come from the salesperson.

◆ Marketing activities to get leads are worthwhile. The key is they have to be expressed in the right language and have a call to action. More marketing dollars should be allocated to getting leads to the sales team than to support sales funnel activity.

◆ Trade shows can be a good source of leads. Most companies do a poor job at working a trade show and talking to attendees at the show with the sole purpose of generating leads at and beyond the show's reach. How many salespeople get a lead from a trade show and call the person who was attending to ask their interest? Less than 20 percent! How many salespeople call that attendee's boss, who allocated money for the attendee to go to the show and involve the boss in a conversation in Russian? Fewer than 5 percent! What a terrible waste.

◆ Prospecting must be a comfortable, unconsciously competent process. If you want to be good at it, you have to do it a lot.

◆ Prospecting must be a part of a sales team's culture. Rewards must be set for good prospecting activities, not just for final revenue results.

◆ Prospecting is mostly a mental attitude, a belief. There are tactics that can be used to be good at it, but salespeople who are good at prospecting believe they are good at it. In reality, they may be mediocre, but if they really believe they are good and constantly work at being good, that enthusiasm comes across to the prospect. Prospecting is easy if you have the right attitude and goals in mind.

◆ Nonverbal communication comes across the phone in volumes. Sit up when you are prospecting at your desk, and smile; the prospect will actually hear that smile in your voice.

◆ Prospecting should be fun. You're contacting people who are going to make you money, and you're going to make them money. It's in the attitude. Have a good time.

Will Someone Give Me a Referral?

The best prospects are referrals. Customer referrals, friend referrals, past customer referrals, web referrals. People will take a phone call from someone they trust.

Salespeople usually feel squeamish asking for a referral. It's kind of like arranging a date for a best friend with someone you don't like.

> "Hey, I wouldn't give a good friend's name to a salesperson. Why would I want to subject them to something like that?"

You as a salesperson may feel that way too, but when you ask a senior-level person for a referral, they like it. As a matter of fact, they look for opportunities to give out referrals.

Collecting Chits

A chit is a short official note, memorandum, or voucher, typically recording a sum owed. Senior executives collect chits, or favors. They barter and swap them all the time, so when they need something, they can call in a chit.

> So when they get the opportunity to pass along a referral of something that worked well for them—your product or service—they love the opportunity, since if you can help out their friend as much as you did them, their friend is going to call them back and say, "Thanks, I owe you one." There's a chit.

Ask more senior people in the organization for referrals. They are collecting chits from their peers and are always looking for an opportunity to get more. Why? Power can be about who you know and what they will do for you, right? Six degrees of separation?

The Prospector's Perspective

Most pro sports players say that to master the sport they play and become the best in the world at it, it is all about mental attitude. In tennis, for example, most of the top twenty tennis pros, men and women, have the shots. They have the physical talent to take them to the top twenty in the world. They say that what is required of them to be number one and stay number one is mental toughness and mental focus. They believe they are great and will win. There is no way they will lose.

Successful prospecting is a mix of homework, talent, and attitude. You have already learned about the homework required of a ProActive salesperson, and you will be getting tools you can use to be better on initial sales calls. Right now, however, it is the attitude that counts. To be a successful salesperson, you must have a positive attitude toward prospecting. What is this right attitude? What's in it for you?

Many salespeople believe that the reason they prospect is to make a sale. This is very straightforward, but it's a nonproductive way to look at prospecting. Remember the goals we laid out on the very first page of this chapter? They're worth repeating:

- ◆ Introduce yourself.
- ◆ Introduce your product/service.
- ◆ Determine if there's an interest in continuing the discussion.

That's it.

Prospecting with the goal of having to make a sale puts a tremendous amount of pressure on you.

"If I don't get this person to call me back, then I won't make a sale, and I won't make my number for the month, then I won't make my quota, then I'll get fired, then I'll be out of work and have to look for a new job . . ."

Salespeople who are good at prospecting have the right prospecting attitude:

"I'm contacting you because I believe you have a need. I may be able to make you money and solve a big problem for you. We might be able to help you satisfy that need. Let's have a conversation to see if there's a mutually beneficial reason for us to start a discussion."

A QUICK REMINDER: A need and the satisfaction of that need are directly dependent on what level you are calling on. Spaniards, Russians, and Greeks have very different needs. They should all be approached in the same manner, but what you say to each should directly relate to their concerns. Speak the right language!

Timing Is All

As we've all learned in our own personal lives, timing is a critical element as well. Even when you address all the right issues, press all the right buttons, speak the right language . . . if the recipient of a prospecting call doesn't need what you have to offer and says "no, thank you"—this does not mean that you shouldn't try again at another time.

Too many salespeople say something like, *"I called him 6 months ago, and there was no interest. I'm not going to waste my efforts on that guy again."* This is a poor prospecting attitude. The timing was not right, but the salesperson has taken it personally and does not have the right prospecting attitude. The right prospecting attitude must be,

"Hi, this is what we do, and based on some homework I have done, this is what you do. Is there a reason for us to get together?"

If the answer is no, and your initial homework is sound, it can be:

♦ Wrong timing: Try again in a month.

♦ Wrong person: You need to find the person with the motivation.

♦   Wrong approach: What language are you speaking? Are you addressing the right issues?

The tactics of placing a well-executed first call are coming up. For now, salespeople must believe. Their attitude must be that they are prospecting to assist both sides mutually.

The Prospect's Perspective—Something to Keep in Mind

If you are prospecting and you have the right attitude, then why is it so hard for prospective customers to agree to spend time with you, especially since you really have the ability to help them out? It's because you are asking the prospect to do something they hate to do. Most salespeople and prospects alike *hate* to change.

You're asking someone to change what they are currently doing, currently evaluating, and currently in process with, and potentially to take a risk. Change takes a lot of work, time, and hassle. People like patterns, repeatability, generalizations, rationalizations, and so on. Who wants more work, which is the work required to change?

Prospects fear change—it carries risk. Your goal is to understand prospects before you make your first contact. Assume that they are skeptical of change, and work *with* them instead of inundating them with Feature/Benefit statements. Understand that their desire to change is low in the beginning of a Buy/Sell process, and start your sales effort from the prospect's perspective, not yours.

The second part of Initiate, the actual sales call, is the next step in the process. You are armed with your homework and are in the right prospecting state of mind, so it's time for your first call.

CHAPTER 5

How to Begin and End Every Sales Call

YOUR HOMEWORK IS DONE, and you're well prepared. You're in the right prospecting frame of mind. You can't stall anymore. It's time to get out there and start selling. It's prospecting time.

The goals of prospecting ("Initiate") were discussed earlier. They are:

- ◆ Introduce yourself (Goal 1)
- ◆ Introduce your product/service (Goal 2)
- ◆ Determine whether to continue on through a Buy/Sell process (Goal 3)

This stage of the sales process is very straightforward and has no "have to get the sale" pressure. If you follow these three goals, your prospecting ability will improve. This is easier said than done, of course, but in this chapter we present some tools that will help you implement the overall goals of the initial call, or in simple terms, prospecting.

Look at the three goals. They all seem very simple in their own right, and they are. The sales novice can execute these goals as easily as the experienced salesperson. The goal that usually gets the most attention is

Goal 2—introducing your product/service. The salesperson gets the most training on this, the most marketing support, and uses this information the most. The thinking is that, if you know the product or service you sell well enough, you can be self-reliant and have to depend only on yourself to earn a living.

But you are spending time learning the least important of the three goals. In-depth product knowledge helps only when you are calling on a User Buyer. At the vice president or CEO level, when you are dealing with a Business Case Buyer, it's all about sales call control, and control of the call is at the beginning and the end: starting off the call in control and directing the prospect to do what you want them to do, and at the end of the call, again getting the prospect to do what you want them to do. The middle, where you have so much knowledge to share, is the filler that you seem never to get quite enough of. Control of the sales call is mastered by flawless execution of Goals 1 and 3.

Goal 1, Introduce yourself, seems on the surface to be very easy, as does Goal 3, Should we continue on through a Buy/Sell process? The intent of these goals is to tell the customer who you are, and at the end, determine whether you have a prospect that is worth your time. Although Goals 1 and 3 seem so simple, so easy, don't lose sight of the fact that it's at these very goals that you'll either win or lose control of this sales call.

Goal 1: Introduce Yourself—The Beginning

At this stage you introduce yourself and try to get the prospect interested enough in what you are saying to start having a conversation with you. For you to be any good at this, you must make a good first impression, whether it's on the phone or in person.

How long do you think you have to make a first impression? Most people would say a minute or two. The answer is between 4 and 6 seconds. In these brief moments, the brain takes information in and starts to filter (generalize, distort, delete) the information it's receiving. A second question is: How long do you think you have to gain or lose credibility? You have roughly between 30 and 40 seconds. After that amount of time, the listener's brain starts asking questions and wants to participate, either positively or negatively. How would you like to be able to, in 30 to 40 seconds:

+ Make a good first impression?
+ Introduce yourself?

- State your business case so the buyer remembers it?
- Get your buyer to agree to your business case?
- Get the buyer's interest and attention?
- Have the buyer begin having a meaningful business discussion with you?

Welcome to the 30-Second Speech

TOOL | The 30-Second Speech™ᵒᵒˡ

The first tool you will learn to prospect successfully with is the 30-Second Speech™ᵒᵒˡ (see Figure 5-1). Many salespeople call this an "elevator speech," but it's much more than that. A good 30-Second Speech is a tool you should use to start out every prospecting sales call. It allows you to start out every prospecting effort in control. A 30-Second Speech should go like this:

"Good morning Mr. Gysin. My name is Mary Jones. I'm with the ABC Company, a leading provider of software and services for sales force automation systems. We provide tools that help salespeople shorten their sales cycles and qualify better. We also help sales managers get to 90 percent forecast accuracy in about half the time. Questions we get all the time from sales VPs like yourself are,

- *"Is there a way to make salespeople more productive without taking them out of the field?"*
- *"Can I really get the maybes out of my funnel that are causing me to spend resources where I shouldn't?" and*
- *"Is there really a way to get my forecasts to 90+ percent accuracy?"*

Before we get into these questions, Mr. Gysin, what are the issues and questions regarding your sales team's productivity that are on your agenda over the next six months?"

This is a 30-Second Speech, and it's a good one. Let's break it down to some basic elements so we can see how to put one together.

Figure 5-1 The 30-Second Speech^{Tool}

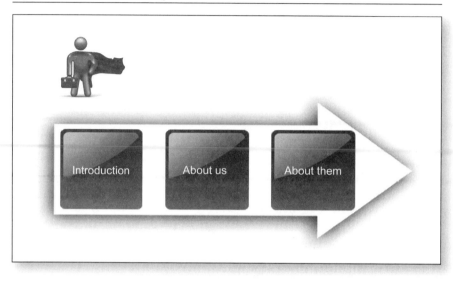

A 30-Second Speech consists of three elements and a conclusion.

Element 1: The Introduction

Simply put, this is where you introduce yourself and your company. This is the time to keep it simple and brief. *"Hi, this is who I am, and this is our company,"* then stop. Right now, there's no need to go any further than that. Here's an example of what you would *not* do:

> "Hi Mr. Jones, my name is Laura Smith and I am the Eastern Region Account Sales Territory Manager for the ABC Division of the XYZ Company, headquartered in Hamilton, New Jersey, and with offices around the world."

Only the salesperson cares about her title and the location of her corporate headquarters. Why would you want to waste someone's time by telling them all about you? They don't care about you; they care about themselves. Get through this Introduction element quickly and easily. You'll have time during the sales call—only if they ask you—to tell them more about yourself or your company. Keep the Introduction short and sweet, so you can get to the messages you need to get into during your 30-Second Speech.

> "Hi, Mr. Jones, my name is Laura Smith, and I'm with the ABC Company."

Element 2: About Us

Now is the time to tell the prospect about you. Keep it short as well, and limited to three things. Why three? Your brain's short-term memory holds seven digits, plus or minus two. This is why we always want things in threes or fives.

Threes:
- ◆ Small/medium/large
- ◆ Good/better/best
- ◆ First, second, third
- ◆ Before/during/after
- ◆ Yesterday/today/tomorrow

Fives:
- ◆ X-small/small/medium/large/X-large
- ◆ A/B/C/D/F (grades in school)
- ◆ Excellent/good/average/poor/very poor

Threes and fives are what people remember, so for Element 2, you want to make an impression with the three things you're going to tell the prospect. (You don't have time to get through five, so stay with three.)

These three things in Element 2 are called *anchors*. What's an anchor? An anchor is something you associate with. For example, answer the following questions:

- ◆ What is the safest car in the world?
- ◆ Who is number one in the car rental business?
- ◆ Where can you go to eat where they have big yellow arches?

If you answered Volvo, Hertz, and McDonald's, you have these as anchors. How do you know that Volvo is the safest car? If you answer, *"Volvo says that they are,"* you are right. Did you know that Volvo has never ranked as the safest car in most automotive magazines?

How do you know that Hertz is number one in the car rental business? Right again, they tell you they are. How do they measure that? Is it by number of cars rented? Number of active rental outlets? Total revenue of the corporation? You don't really know, but what you do know is that they are number one. Who is number two in the car rental business? You probably answered Avis. How do you know they are number two? Because they try harder? How do they try harder? Do they run after you when you check your car in? Smile larger? What do they do? You don't know, you just know they try harder.

The list of great anchors goes on and on. Anchors are very powerful, and you may want to develop some for your company. You want to have a list of between ten and twenty anchors available for a 30-Second Speech, so you can use the one that's right for the specific call you are making. Usually, your anchors won't change too often, but when you're speaking to a CEO, for instance, have CEO-type anchors ready. It will keep their interest and let them know right up front they should continue paying attention to you.

Element 3: About Them

After you create three brief anchors about you, you want to shift the discussion to the prospect because, quite frankly, it's all about them. You want to now interest the prospect in terms they can understand and get them interested enough to start a discussion. Remember, your goal is to have the prospect interested and to build enough rapport during the prospecting call so a basic business discussion can begin.

It's now time to capture enough of the prospect's interest so they start to have a conversation with you, from which you can determine the appropriateness of a next step with this client. For you to accomplish both these objectives—getting their interest and getting them involved with the conversation—Element 3 must be in a question format.

Questions get the prospect to think. If they are good questions, which mean ones relevant to the prospect, they will think:

> *"Yes, these are questions I ask myself all the time. Perhaps this person really understands my issues."*
>
> *"Yes, these are some of my issues, and there are some other ones I really would like to have the answers to as well. This person is in the right ballpark; maybe they have some answers."*
>
> *"No, these are not the questions I ask myself, but they're pretty close. Let's talk about it."*

Any way you look at it, the prospect has to think and get involved when you are asking questions. Now you must determine:

1. What are these "good and relevant" questions?
2. What kind of questions should you ask?

The answer to the first question is easy. You've already done some homework on this prospect based upon the topics you uncovered in the previous chapters. Use this homework effort to formulate great questions. It doesn't take that long and can be well worth the time to find out what the prospect is about before you make that first call. The other area to formulate your questions from is provided by the Three Languages^{Tool} in Chapter 3. You already know what is important to what level of buyer. Assume for an instance you are calling a vice president (and why would you be calling any lower on a first call?). What's important to a vice president? It's Value of course; increase revenue and decrease cost. So assemble your questions around the ValueStar (also from Chapter 3—love that chapter!). Ask questions about ROI, Time, and Risk. Find out what the company is doing to become more competitive so they make more money, and ask questions in these areas. What you'll find out after a while is that all vice presidents (Russians), have similar issues; it's why they speak the same language—Value. Once you get good at this, the questions will start to flow with very little homework.

The second question—what kind of questions do you ask?—is easier than the previous question. Remember, it's all about them. They are interested in themselves, and not in you yet. They don't care about you. So ask the classic WIIFM questions.

WIIFM Questions—Questions That Are on the Prospect's Mind

"How can I increase revenue in the short term with little or no further investment?"

"How can I get my product to market faster than I am currently on track to do?"

"Is there a way to lower my risk on the key two or three decisions I am making over the next six months?"

Element 3 asks questions. Questions get the prospect involved and motivated to talk with you. It's why they will allow you to talk with them, because they have questions. It goes to the Law of Questions.

THE LAW OF QUESTIONS

No executive or prospect will ever agree to meet with you because you have something to tell them. They don't care. They'll only agree to meet with you because they have a question they need an answer to. Get their question out, not your information in.

Ask great questions that will get their questions and issues out on the table, and then start a dialog; this means they must be WIIFM questions.

The transition between Element 2 and Element 3 is called a *bridge* (see Figure 5-2). You have to create a bridge between Element 2 and 3 to transition to the questions. Bridge phrases can be:

"Executives like yourself are always asking us . . ."

"Companies we talk to want to know . . ."

"Major clients like yourself often wonder . . ."

"People in your position frequently ask us . . ."

"Some homework I have done on your company shows you are probably asking yourself . . ."

Figure 5-2 30-Second Speech[Tool] **with Bridge**

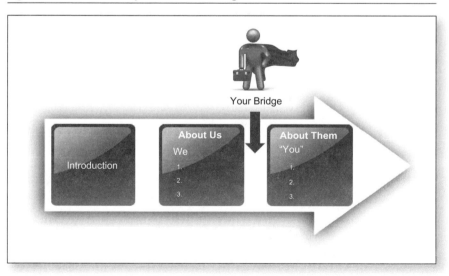

"You are probably wondering . . ."
"You probably ask yourself on a daily basis . . ."

Use whatever bridge phrase you feel comfortable with. It doesn't really matter which one you use; it matters that you have a bridge phrase, and it must be in question form. If it's not a question, if it's a statement, it has less of a chance of starting a conversation. Remember:

Statements = Agree/Disagree
Questions = Answers and Conversation

Putting together the three elements of a 30-Second Speech now sounds like this:

Element 1: Introduction
Good morning, Mr. Gysin. My name is Mary Jones. I'm a salesperson for the ABC Company.

Element 2: About Us
At ABC

1. *We are a leading provider of software and services for sales force automation solutions.*

2. *We provide tools that help salespeople shorten their sales cycles and qualify prospects better.*

3. *We also help sales managers get more than 90 percent forecast accuracy in about half the time.*

Element 3: Bridge Phrase
Many of the questions we get from sales VPs like yourself are:

1. *"Is there a way to make salespeople more productive without having to take them out of the field?"*

2. *"Can I really get the maybes out of my funnel that are causing me to spend resources where I shouldn't?"*

3. *"Is there really a way to get my forecasts to 90+ percent accuracy?"*

> **Summarize and Flip**
> Before we get into these questions, Mr. Gysin, what are the issues and questions regarding your sales team's productivity that are on your agenda over the next six months?

Notice that we have brought a new element into the discussion, the Flip^{Tool}.

TOOL   **Flip**^{Tool}

Summarize and Flip is the way you end the speech (see Figure 5-3). You summarize the questions you have asked, and then use the Flip tool. A Flip is a tool to get the prospect to start talking. A Flip is asking a question that the prospect must answer. You need to Flip at the end of a 30-Second Speech so the prospect starts talking. Flipping is one of the top five characteristics of a top salesperson, as outlined in *ProActive Sales Management, Second Edition* (AMACOM, 2009). Flipping is remembering to ask questions so the prospect gets involved and starts to talk. Flipping makes sure the prospect feels included, and that the salesperson begins to do the listening.

There you have the schematics of a good 30-Second Speech introduction. Some basic rules are:

1. You can't just jump in with a 30-Second Speech. There will usually be a few moments of idle conversation. Pace yourself. Examples of introductions are, *"Is this a good time for you"* (the permission call) or, *"Mr. Patel asked me to call you"* (the reference call), or *"I was doing some homework on your company and discovered there may be a reason . . ."* (the homework call). Whatever your style is, use an introduction you feel comfortable with.

2. E-mail 30-Second Speeches also work very well. Just keep the focus on the prospect and remember to Summarize and Flip.

3. Keep with the *I-We-You* perspectives. Start with *I*, then go to *we*, then finish up with *you*. When you go from Element 2 to Element 3, you cross the Your Bridge. Once you cross the Your Bridge, use only *you* and *we*, but never *I* (unless you are paraphrasing in a WIIFM question).

Figure 5-3 30-Second Speech^{Tool}: Summarize and Flip

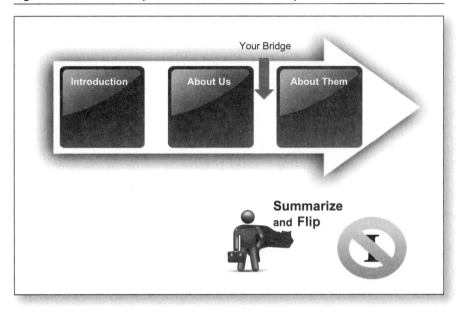

4. In this book, we are asking you to go Intro-3–3-Summarize and Flip. In the real world, you may go Intro-2–2-Summarize and Flip, or Intro-2–3-Summarize and Flip. Of course, you never want to go to Intro-3–1-Summarize and Flip, since that puts the attention on you and not on the prospect, and you want to put the attention on them, right?

Write your 30-Second Speech right now.

The 30-Second Speech is the tool that gives you a process by which you communicate during the prospecting part of selling. It supplies you with the confidence to give a prospect an overview of what you do and what's in it for them powerfully and concisely. It will allow you to have many different options for whatever language you need to speak and for any situation. Finally, it keeps you focused on the prospect; this is what the prospect wants, and as a ProActive salesperson, you oblige. Use, practice, and perfect the 30-Second Speech (see Figure 5-4). Make it your own, and watch the results.

Questions, Questions, Questions

The Initial Interest phase of the Buy/Sell process cannot be complete without a discussion of questions. The Law of Questions says an executive

Figure 5-4 30-Second Speech^{Tool} Exercise

Hi, I'm _____with: _____

What we do is:

* _____

* _____

* _____

We are getting a lot of questions, like:

* _____

* _____

* _____

These are great questions, but first, what are your challenges and what risks do you see to *your* organization over the next few months?

will agree to meet with you only because that executive has a question. It's up to you to ask questions to get the prospect's issues on the table so a discussion can take place. This is very important.

Sales management spends a great deal of time training their salespeople on product knowledge so that when they get in front of a prospect, usually a manager, they can spew out what they know. There are even names for this phenomenon: Spray and Pray, Show up and Throw up, and Technicolor Yawn. Reactive salespeople disgorge product knowledge and do it with enthusiasm. They have PowerPoint slides, handouts, and brochures, all in the name of "educating" the customer. This is great. There will be a time when education is important, but ProActive salespeople know that great questions are not just something they can think up at the spur of the moment. Like anything else, they need to be practiced.

Practice great questions. How? Be the customer.

When you are doing your homework, put yourself in the customer's chair. Physically move across your desk and into a customer chair if you have to. Ask yourself, "If I were the customer, what would be important to me right now? What is keeping me awake at night?" If you were the prospect, would you really be asking yourself, "How would I use this salesperson's product or service?" They don't even know about your product or service. They don't care at the moment. It's all about them.

Questions will win the day, and you need to have done your homework to figure out the questions that are on your prospect's mind? You need to write them down and have a discussion with your boss or with another sales associate about the questions you're planning to ask. Practicing great questions will give you an advantage and stop you from executing the "Show up and Throw up" sales model when you are on the call.

Asking Great Questions

A ProActive sales manager relays the following story.

Some years ago, when I had just been hired as the national account manager for a large corporation, I went on an initial sales call with one of the reps, Dennis. He had a surprisingly good sales record, in spite of his unprofessional dress and overly casual manner. The call was going well, and I was letting Dennis do all the selling. Halfway through the meeting, however, Dennis was starting to drive me crazy. The senior person in the room was asking questions, and Dennis was not answering them. The senior person would ask, "*So what can your system do to solve this one particular problem?*" The answer was obvious. We could do what the executive wanted to do, and do it very well. Dennis's response would be, "*That's a good question. Why would you want to do that?*" or, "*That's a good question. How would you want the system to handle that?*" It was driving me nuts. Finally, after about 10 minutes into this questioning session, I decided to get involved. After all, it was my right as the national account manager. I started jumping in with:

"*Mr. Smith, we can do that, and we do that this way.*"
"*Mr. Smith, we have done that for many clients, and we can do that for you.*"
"*Mr. Smith, that's a good question. The answer is, yes, we can.*"

I thought I was brilliant. We finished up the call, and as we were driving away, I asked Dennis what he had been doing. Why on earth, when asked a question by the senior person in the room, did he not show how we could address it?

He turned to me very calmly and said,

> "What makes you think he wanted an answer? Usually, I find that when they ask a question, they have an answer in mind. I always figured that if I could get them to answer their own question, they take ownership of my solution, and I usually get the sale."

I instantly realized that Dennis was absolutely right. I needed to put away my ego.

I learned a great lesson that day. Ask great questions, have the customer figure out the answer to how you can help them, have ownership transfer, and you win. You do this by asking great questions, not by having great answers.

Goal 2: Introduce Your Product/Service—The Middle

In this part of the call you tell the prospect about your product/service. Feature/Benefit statements are the rule, and this part of the call follows three rules:

1. Always follow a feature with a benefit—what is in it for them?
2. Use multimedia and multiple formats to convey your message and to keep the introduction alive. It can be PowerPoint slides, flip charts, brochures, testimonials, or catalogs.
3. Keep the customers involved. The more they are involved with the introduction, the more they will get excited.

Goal 3: Do We Continue on Through a Buy/Sell Process?—The End

The purpose of Goal 3 is to end with you in control. It is time for a tool that lets you end every meeting professionally, ProActively, and with you in control.

TOOL   Summarize, Bridge, and Pull™

Determining whether you want to continue on through a Buy/Sell process is the third goal of the Initiate sales call. The 30-Second Speech is how you start a call and address the first goal. The Summarize,

Bridge, and Pull™ (SBP) is how you end every call and address the last goal. Every call has to end with an SBP. Here is an example of an SBP:

> "Well Mr. Gysin, it sounds like we accomplished a lot today. You said you wanted to increase your revenue by getting your products through the development cycle 20 percent faster, as well as increasing the flexibility you have in your packaging and lowering your overall engineering costs by 10 percent, and we discussed how we might be able to help. Would you agree?"
>
> "Yes, I would. It has been a good meeting."
>
> "Great. So a good next step should be to sit down together, so we can learn more about what you want to accomplish, and you can learn more about what we do. At that point, you will be in a perfect position to determine whether we should go any further with this conversation. Does that sound good to you?"

This is a well-executed SBP. You need to take it apart to see the structure and then build it back up. A well-executed SBP has three parts:

1. You/I
2. Bridge Question
3. Next Step

You/I

This is where you summarize the discussion you just had, making sure you put the prospect's position first. Never put *I* first; it is a Buy/Sell cycle, not the other way around. Start with an introductory statement, and then go right for a "You position" statement.

Intro Statement

"Well Mr. Gysin, it sounds like we accomplished a lot today.

You: *You said you wanted to increase your revenue through getting your products through the development cycle 20 percent faster, as well as increasing the flexibility you have in your packaging and lowering your overall engineering costs by 10 percent.*

I: *We discussed how we might be able to help.*

Bridge Question

Here the salesperson prepares the prospect to go across the bridge with him or her. This is not losing control, because you are the one proposing the bridge question.

> *"Do you agree?"*
>
> *"Do you have any questions?"*
>
> *"We talked about that one thing a few minutes ago. Have we covered all the points?"*

You must now ask the prospect about the meeting itself, since asking about *you* or *I* is one-dimensional, whereas asking about the meeting is inclusive: *"Do you agree that it's been a good meeting (or a good conversation), Mr. Gysin?*

The buyer usually agrees because it is a summation of the conversation that just took place. You want him or her to agree that he or she had a good meeting or conversation; don't ask for agreement on the issues at this point. They are agreeing that they said this, you said that, and it sounds pretty good right now. The prospect agrees to this because he or she was in the same conversation you were in, and you both have the same perspective of the meeting.

The prospect must agree. If the prospect does *not* agree, then you have uncovered an objection that you need to deal with. It's much better to uncover an objection early in the Buy/Sell process than to let it emerge later, after you have invested a lot more time and energy.

Next Step

This is when you propose the next step in the Buy/Sell process.

> **Next Step**
>
> *"Great. So a good next step should be to sit down together, so we can learn more about what you want to accomplish and you can learn more about what we do. At that point, you will be in a perfect position to determine whether we should go any further with this conversation. Does that sound good to you?"*

In most cases, the prospect agrees since it is a natural next step in the process. You have completed an SBP and are in control of this sales call and this deal.

An SBP must be done after every meeting, after every conversation. It's very easy to lose control of a deal. It can happen in a split second, usually at the end of a meeting, when a prospect takes over and sends the deal in a different direction than you want it to go. You think it's just a detour, but it's not; it is a battle for control. An SBP is a tool to be used at the end of every sales call to keep control every step of the way.

Prospects want to be led, so you must be the one who does the leading. In the role-playing we do in our training seminars, we have salespeople take on the buyer's role. At the end of every role-play scenario, we ask the salespeople who acted the parts of the buyers what they thought of the role-playing. You can consistently depend on the salesperson who is in the role of the buyer to say something like:

> "The things I noticed the most were the beginning and the end. If the role-play started out with a 30-Second Speech, I felt good, like I knew what the agenda was and what the purpose of the meeting was. When the role-play ended with a Summarize, Bridge, and Pull, I felt like we were working together and it was a logical next step.
>
> "When there was no 30-second speech, I was busy thinking what am I here for, what's the point, what's the agenda, and what's the context of this conversation? I was thinking these things rather than listening to the salesperson. I wanted to know what the purpose of the meeting was, and we never really got to it. I got more and more annoyed during the call because I did not know the purpose of the call. I was not really listening to the sales pitch.
>
> "Worse, though, was when there was no Summarize, Bridge, and Pull. I ended up telling the salesperson what to do next, and I lost confidence in him. I felt he did not know what to do next, so I proposed a next step, and I usually proposed a next step without me in it, since I wasn't needed, and I could delegate it to other people on my staff. By the way, the salesperson was happy to take my reference and delegation down a level too. He assumed it was a way to get into the organization, do some work, and then get back to me. Trust me, I was not going to let him get back in."

Summarize, Bridge, and Pull is a way to make sure you are in control at the end of the meeting. Too often, salespeople leave a sales meeting thinking they are in control, when in actuality someone else is pulling the strings. Here are some typical mistakes salespeople make at the end of a sales call:

Salespeople's Top Five Mistakes (aka "Things NOT to Do")

1. Ask the prospect what to do next. This is the classic case of a salesperson not being prepared with a next step. The salesperson thinks that if he does what the prospect tells him to do, then at the end, the prospect will give him the order. This is sales at its reactionary worst.

2. Follow the prospect's requested next step. Being led by someone else is another classic sales mistake. The Law of Sales Control says the buyer is always neutral. If you are not controlling the sales process, someone else is, and usually that someone else does not have your best interest in mind.

3. Do what the prospect asks you to do. This is similar to the preceding scenario, but here the prospect has detailed his or her entire buy process, usually a formal one, and a salesperson believes if he or she can follow the prospect's process better than anyone else, he or she will win the deal. This thinking is wrong because it is not the salesperson's process to begin with, and will not be their process in the end. The salesperson who put the process together will own the deal.

In many cases, prospects can make you feel like they are working with you on their process, so you feel you have a leg up. You have to understand that they are making the salespeople from other companies feel that way too.

4. Try an SBP, then do what the prospect wants. A salesperson tries an SBP, and the buyer says he or she agrees, but would rather do something else. Then the salesperson agrees to do what the prospect wants to do and leaves the proposed next step hanging.

> "Well Mr. Gysin, it sounds like we accomplished a lot today. You said you wanted to increase your revenue by getting your products through the development cycle 20 percent faster, as well as increasing the flexibility you have in your packaging and lowering your overall engineering costs by 10 percent, and we discussed how we might be able to help, would you agree?"
>
> "Yes, I would. It has been a very good meeting."

"Great. So a good next step should be to sit down together so we can learn more about what you want to accomplish, and you can learn more about what we do. At that point, you will be in a perfect position to determine whether we should go any further with this conversation. Does that sound good to you?"

"That sounds good, but first I want you to talk with Bob and Mary" (two managers, Spaniards of course).

At this point the salesperson has a choice. He or she can agree with the prospect and go talk to Bob and Mary. In some cases, the salesperson is delighted to go talk to Bob and Mary because he or she now has a reference.

"Hi Bob, Mr. Gysin, your boss, told me to call you . . ."

This is quite a weapon, except it is useless because the prospect is now in control of the sale. Your tactic should be to agree with the prospect, and then gain control back.

"Yes, that sounds good. I will have a discussion with Bob and Mary by the end of the week. Let's then get back together, discuss the findings of that conversation, and then you and I can decide whether we should go any further, since there is no way I am leaving this meeting with you in control." (You may want to leave off the last bit and just think it, not say it.)

5. Use the Summarize and Pull tool, with no Bridge. This is all salesperson and no prospect involvement—an easy trap to fall in, and can ruin a sale.

"Well Mr. Gysin, it sounds like we accomplished a lot today. You said you wanted to increase your revenue by getting your products through the development cycle 20 percent faster, as well as increasing the flexibility you have in your packaging and lowering your overall engineering costs by 10 percent, and we discussed how we might be able to help (no Bridge), *so I think a good next step should be where...*"

A Bridge Question is always needed. You must walk hand in hand with the prospect across the Bridge. Going across first, then yelling to the prospect to come along after you are already across, is not a mutual sales process, and the prospect will feel he or she "getting sold to." You must have a Bridge phrase:

> *"Would you agree?"*
> *"Does this sound about right?"*
> *"Is this what you thought we covered today?"*
> *"Are we of the same opinion on this?"*
> *"Do you concur?"*

Use what seems natural, but do use a Bridge. This is a mutual Buy/Sell process, and you must always Bridge to a Next Step, not just go across the Bridge yourself and hope the prospect follows you.

Summarize, Bridge, and Pull is a powerful tool in the salesperson's repertoire. You'll get to a point where you'll feel strange if you *don't* use an SBP in a meeting. That will be a good sign, since without an SBP, control of the sales process is up for grabs. Be good, be ProActive, and use the SBP tool to stay in control of every meeting and every sale.

This chapter has presented a lot of material on how the ProActive salesperson can own that first sales call, but we have a few other prospecting tricks up our sleeve. Read on!

CHAPTER 6

Additional Sales Call Introductions

TAILORING THE SKILLS YOU USE with 30-Second Speech™, described in Chapter 5, for voice mail and e-mail is not hard. The key is to adapt them for the right type of sales communication.

Voice Mail

When most salespeople leave a voice mail, they do a good job at the introduction and anchors. Then they ask for a callback but forget the WIIFM questions, which is why they are getting a low callback ratio.

Additionally, salespeople, trying to ensure that they give enough information to create an interest for the prospect to call back, tend to leave messages that are too long, reducing their effectiveness. The result, again, is a low callback ratio. The solution to both these problems is to tailor the 30-Second Speech into a 20-Second Speech for voice mails.

Figure 6-1 20-Second Help Speech^{Tool}

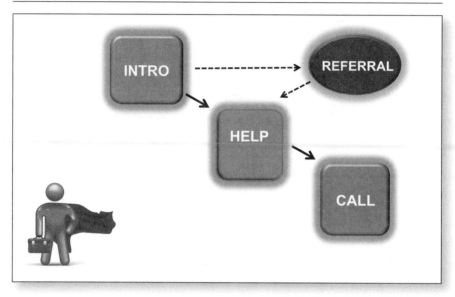

The 20-Second Speeches

There are two 20-second speeches tailored for a voice-mail: the 20-Second Help Speech™ (see Figure 6-1) and the 20-Second Pattern Interrupt Speech™.

TOOL | **20-Second Help Speech™**

This is what you hear: *"Please leave a message at the tone, and I'll get back to you as soon as I can."* This is what you say after the beep: *"Hello Mr. Jarvis, my name is Bill Barret from the ABC Company, and I could really use your help. Please call me back at 432.456.7890."*

That's the simple "I need your help" speech. It has three components:

1. **Introduction:** You state your name and your company. No more, no less. (Don't forget the name of your company, otherwise the prospect will be wondering who you are, and will be unlikely to call back.)

2. **Call for help:** Keep it simple. Don't give a reason for why you are looking for help, just ask for it.

3. **Request action:** Tell the prospect where to call you back.

Here's why this short speech works.

♦ You'll be surprised how many people want to help.
♦ Don't add what you do or any other information; keep to the script.
♦ Be sincere; really ask for their help.
♦ It's a legitimate call. When the prospect calls you back, just ask for directions. Yes, ask for directions.

> *"This is Bill Barret returning your call. You need my help?"*
>
> *"Yes, sir, thank you for returning my call. The reason I called is I'm with the ABC Company, the leader in the high-speed offset printing market. We are currently saving companies about 30 percent on their overall printing costs, and I was calling you to find out who in your company would be responsible for looking into something like this? Would that be you, or someone else in your organization?"*
>
> *"That would be me. How can I help you?"*

Once you've opened the conversation, you've introduced yourself and started building rapport.

This 20-Second Help Speech is probably the tool in ProActive Selling about which most salespeople have their doubts. How can something so simple be effective? As we have consistently documented for a number of years, companies that use this 20-Second Speech format have a 30+ percent callback ratio. Why? Because people generally want to help.

If you want, you can add a referral to this speech. Add the name of someone who would cause rapport to be built. It could be an acquaintance, a co-worker, or perhaps a prominent person in the industry. You can even mention someone who works for them, which will ensure their curiosity. Just don't lie. Don't use the name of someone you don't really know. It's easier than you think to check on your referral.

TOOL	20-Second Pattern Interrupt Speech™

The second voice mail speech is called the 20-Second Pattern Interrupt Speech (see Figure 6-2).

"Please leave a message at the tone, and I'll get back to you as soon as I can."

Beep.

"Hello Mr. Jarvis, my name is Bill Barret from the ABC Company, a leader in the offset printing market. The purpose of my call is I'm talking to a lot of VPs of Manufacturing right now, and I'm getting questions like:

♦ 'How can I increase production without increasing costs?' and
♦ 'How can I get faster delivery times than I'm getting today so I don't fall behind schedule because of ink?'

If these are questions you are looking at, please give me a call at 432.456.7890 and let's discuss your potential options."

Figure 6-2 20-Second Pattern Interrupt Speech™

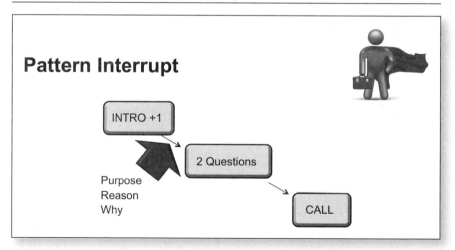

The 20-second Pattern Interrupt Speech breaks down into these communication elements:

1. **Introduction Plus 1:** State your name and one feature of who you are or what your company does. This will last about 3 or 4 seconds, just about the time the prospect has heard enough and is going to make a judgment call on listening to more, or deleting this message.

2. **Pattern Interrupt:** This is where you interrupt the pattern, since the prospect is probably going to delete your message right about now.

   "The purpose of my call . . ."
   "The reason for my call . . ."
   "Why I'm calling is . . ."

   Have you ever gone to a lecture, and right at about the 20-minute mark, you are ready to fall asleep, and the speaker says:

   ". . . and in conclusion . . ."
   ". . . and in summary . . ."
   ". . . and finally . . ."

   That wakes you up. It interrupts the pattern of the speech. You listen more intently to anything after a pattern interrupt. So use the words *reason, why, purpose,* or anything else you can think of at the 3–4-second mark to break the usual voice mail pattern, and accentuate the word . . . it creates the interrupt.

3. **Two Questions:** Nothing transfers ownership and gets someone thinking like good questions. Use two here, and not the usual three from the 30-Second Speech, since on a voice mail, you have less time to be effective.

These two 20-Second Speeches, the Help and the Pattern Interrupt, will get your prospect to call you back. These tools provide a great way to get those sales calls started.

E-Mails

E-mails are becoming less effective due to the overload of spam and the corresponding abundance of increasingly more efficient spam filters. Be selective in your e-mail prospecting. Use e-mail only when it's appropriate to the situation, like when you want to include a link or an attachment. Many people are now attaching a link to a short video (keep it to 20 to 30 seconds) so the e-mail can come to life if the prospect so desires.

When you do send prospecting e-mails, follow these rules:

1. E-mails should be informative. What would catch the prospect's eye? Subject lines that are all about you and your company are ineffective, unless you are Apple, Google, or the President of the United States.

2. E-mails should require the prospect to take some sort of action. Ask the prospect to click back, respond, or go to a different place on the Web. Having the prospect take action will get them started in the transfer of ownership process.

3. Prospecting e-mails should be brief and extremely focused. Specifically, they should contain no more than five paragraphs, with no more than three sentences (*short* sentences, please) per paragraph. One of the paragraphs should have bullets, and there should be three bullets, two in AWAY language (remember the TOWARDS/AWAY^{Tool}, from Chapter 1?).

4. The subject line must arouse the prospect's interest. For example, if you are selling to a VP of sales, the subject line should achieve one of the following:

- Cause curiosity ("Look what happened in the last quarter").
- Ask a question ("Are you tired of always being behind the hiring curve?").
- Provide new information ("The top 10 things VPs of sales are doing for the next year").
- Create a reference ("VPs of sales in consumer medical devices are speaking out").
- Provide a path ("The next step you need to take for a free trip . . .").

5. A picture is worth a thousand words; a video clip, ten thousand! Include a picture if you can, or add a link to a video, even if it's only a 30-second clip of you inviting the prospect to get in touch with you.

E-mails can also be a way to continue a conversation and can be a very useful, relatively painless (and not at all pushy) way to keep something moving. Asking the prospect to take even the smallest action step will keep a sale moving.

The biggest problem with an e-mail (assuming you have grabbed the prospect's attention and gotten her to read it) is that it's a one-way communication document and does not allow two-way conversation. A phone call—or a WebEx/Skype/GoToMeeting/etc. contact—is almost always better.

A Word of Warning

Only IM if you have a very strong relationship with the prospect. It may enable instantaneous communication, and is more personal than e-mail—but IMs are considered by many to be intrusive. This is especially true of Russians and Greeks, who cannot afford to be easily accessible!

Let the prospect initiate this mode of communication. If he says, *"IM me with those new figures as soon as you work them up,"* do so; but don't go on to flood him with a constant stream of "hot-off-the-press" information.

Finally, the second or third prospecting e-mail should have some humor. Tasteful humor can make you more personable and set you apart. Examples:

♦ Trying to reach you is harder than getting my kids to call me back.

♦ Please let me know if you want to have a quick conversation regarding your challenges in the next few quarters. I promise I'll listen.

♦ Please hit the reply button. It's that little blue thing on the screen right now and you can use it.

Launching a sales conversation with a prospect is not difficult once you understand the way to do it effectively. Don't improvise or try to speak off-the-cuff. 30-Second Speeches, 20-Second Speeches, and e-mails are great ways to start a conversation. Use some of the tools presented here to be ProActive and more effective.

Beyond the First Call

Although that first call is extremely important, every call offers similar opportunity, and challenges. You can modify the 30-Second Speech™ to serve you at every contact with the prospect (see Figure 6-3).

TOOL | **30-Second Speech: Second Call and Beyond**™

Every meeting or presentation, not just a prospecting call, should start out with a 30-Second Speech. The 30-Second Speech format—Intro-3-3-Summarize and Flip—never changes. Only the contents will change for every sales call and presentation, after the initial call.

For you to use a 30-Second Speech on calls after the first one, you should modify it so it becomes more effective. Here's how it works:

30-Second Speech	First Speech	All Other Sales Calls
Opening	Introduction	Introduction
Second Element	About us	Last time we talked . . .
Third Element	About them	Your agenda/concerns/ issues were . . .
Closing	Summarize and Flip	If good meeting today, Next Step/t

The Second, Third, and Closing elements change to fit the circumstance of the meeting, which allows you to leverage the 30-Second Speech tool on every sales call.

Change the second element to restate what the prospect's goals are. *"Last time we met, you said you want to:*

1. *Increase production by 10 percent,*

2. *Lower costs by 5 percent, and*

3. *Get the new product out 30 days faster."*

At this point, the prospect is saying to themselves, *"That's exactly what I said. These folks were taking good notes. They heard me."*

The third element is now why you are meeting. You say, *"So today, we are going to:*

Figure 6-3 30-Second Speech: Second Call and Beyond[Tool]

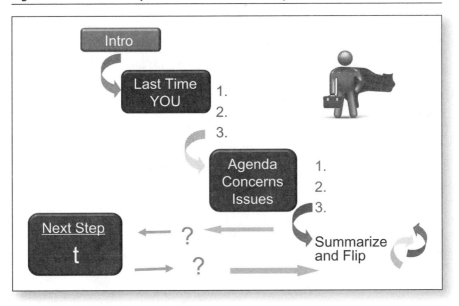

1. *Cover the pricing options for you to consider,*

2. *Discuss that one point you brought up last time. I think we have some good answers for you there, and*

3. *Talk about availability delivery windows.*

Then you validate with a question, *"Is that right? Are you OK with this agenda?"*

Once you have validated the agenda, instead of going right to the things you have put together for this meeting, you need to get a commitment from the prospect that we are all thinking about continuing the Buy/Sell process together. You do this by closing the 30-Second Speech with a conditional question:

> "Great, so let's get started with today's meeting. But before we do, I want to make sure that if we are in agreement today, and all goes well, then a good next step would be for us to validate what we know so far, and we can do that with a demonstration of the product by next Wednesday. *Is that OK with you folks?"*

IMPORTANT SECRET TIP: Note that the salesperson says "next Wednesday." This was not a random act. It's vital to mention a definite time as you introduce the Next Step—and that little "t" in the Next Step box on Figure 6-3 is there to remind you.

You want to do this so you can be ProActively in control of this entire call. Without you offering the next step and getting agreement on it before the meeting starts, you'll start the meeting, give everything you have to the prospect, including control . . . they have what they need. Asking them for a next step at the *end* of the meeting, with the prospect in control, gives the prospect the ability to say, *"We'll get back to you."*

By asking for the next step before the meeting starts, *you* are in control. If the prospect objects to the next step (*"No that's not really what we had in mind, but let's get to the meeting today, okay?"*), you have a battle for control on your hands. It's at this point where you get that control back.

> "Sure, but it seems like a logical next step if this meeting goes well. What were your thoughts on a next step?"

Which gives you the chance at discussing their objections before you give all your hard work away, and you are left with nothing. Too much objecting at this point by the prospect may signal a disqualification issue.

The Second Call and Beyond version of the 30-Second Speech usually takes somewhat longer than 30 seconds (anywhere from 1 to 3 minutes), because you are inputting customer goals and objectives and trying to gain agreement on a next step before the meeting starts. It's called a 30-Second Speech nonetheless, because it follows that format so directly.

In the role-plays that we use in our ProActive Sales training seminars, top salespeople get a chance to write, use, and listen to 30-Second Speeches. These role-plays always led to three conclusions:

1. Most 30-Second Speeches came across very well, regardless of how salespeople believe that they delivered it.

2. Top salespeople were doing something close to a 30-Second Speech already, but not as powerful and leverageable. With practice, they became more proficient and comfortable with the 30-Second Speech and were able to easily incorporate the speech into their sales toolbox.

3. When the salesperson was the buyer in the role-plays, they actually liked this modified 30-Second Speech for the second meeting and beyond better than the original, since it proposes an outcome, a "next step" in this very first minute of the meeting. If the prospect agrees, then all the salesperson has to do is execute on the agenda of the meeting, and does not have to worry about taking control at the end, since the next step has already been established. Even if, during the meeting, the next step needs to change, the salesperson can begin with the next step to which the parties agreed at the beginning of the meeting. A salesperson might say,

"It seems we have had a good meeting. We agreed earlier that if today's meeting went well, our next step was going to be . . ."

The beginning of a sales presentation is all about setting the agenda and controlling the content and tempo of the meeting. A 30-Second Speech opening, followed by a discussion of the Agenda/Concerns/Issues outlined in the 30-Second Speech, is the most powerful way to begin a sales call or presentation, either in person or over the phone. Whether this follow-up lasts a few minutes or up to half of the entire meeting, the 30-Second Speech is a professional way to set the agenda and control the meeting.

It is a simple, clean, and winning formula.

You've done a great job. You've set up the sale and are in control. ProActively. Now, let's get into the heart of the Buy/Sell process.

CHAPTER 7

Control the Middle and the End

WITH ALL YOUR TRAINING AND EXPERIENCE, you probably do a good job of sales education already. Add the following tools to your toolbox so that you become even better (used for sales education, these three tools will help you stay in control):

- Ask 'em/Tell 'em/Ask 'em^{Tool}
- GAP Chart^{Tool}
- SalesMap^{Tool}

But before we look at these new tools, let's talk about how you can make educational sales meetings truly ProActive.

Turn Sales Education into ProActive Sales Presentations

Most companies have their own philosophies on sales presentations. Some prefer to do demonstrations; others would rather stick to PowerPoint slides or "decks," and still others would rather review technical or marketing literature. Style and company philosophies can be very important in the sales education process when delivering product/ service features and benefits.

What is just as critical as features and benefits in the sales presentations are the tactics of the sales presentation. You need to look at ways you can improve your sales education tactics and make your sales presentations ProActive.

The goal of sales education is to create a two-way flow of information. First, you must set the stage for the attainment of this goal. Reactive salespeople typically walk into the meeting room, take out their laptop computers, plug them into a computer projection system, turn off the lights, and start with a 30-plus slide presentation. The presentation lasts 20 to 40 minutes, the computer goes off, the lights come on, and the salesperson asks, "Are there any questions?" This is not a two-way education meeting. In a slightly better scenario, the salesperson begins with the lights on, discusses an agenda for 5 minutes, dives into the presentation, answers a few questions that are all about the product or service presented, then turns on the lights at the end.

The phone sales presentation follows the same format. After a good 30-second speech, the agenda is set, and the prospect starts to talk. As soon as the prospect begins talking, the reactive salesperson goes into answer mode, trying to formulate answers so that as soon as there is a pause in the discussion, he or she can jump in and start "selling."

It is time to give your sales education process an overhaul and make it effective in terms of the prospect. The delivery tactics of sales presentations need to be refined. It does not matter if you think that yours is good; what matters is whether it's good from the prospect's point of view. These ProActive prospect-focused tactics that we discuss below are what you need work on, because "it's all about them."

There are three parts of a sales presentation that need to be addressed to make a sales education presentation ProActive.

1. The Beginning: Setting the Stage
2. The Middle: Them–Us–Them Presentations
3. The Ending: The Mutual Agreement to a Next Step

Note that these parts are similar to the three parts of generating Initial Interest.

Part 1: The Beginning—Setting the Stage

The beginning of every sales call, of every sales presentation, is crucial. It sets the stage for the entire meeting, informs everyone of the agenda, and gets all the important issues on the table, especially issues that have occurred in the *prospect's* world since the last meeting that the salesperson knows nothing about.

Many things happen in between sales calls, and all too often the prospect suddenly interrupts a salesperson—mid-meeting—and says:

> "Gayle, this is good, but some things have changed that you need to know about before you continue."

Unless you have set the stage properly, the prospect most likely won't speak up before the meeting starts. Instead of addressing his current concerns, you will end up wasting half the meeting on topics that are now of no interest to him.

Part 2: The Middle—Them–Us–Them Presentations

The middle part of the sales presentation is really the content part of the meeting. It's the discussion of features, benefits, and the value your products and services are going to be delivering, and you are highlighting why the prospect should buy from you. For this middle part of sales presentations to be effective and ProActive, it must be interesting to the prospect. How do you prepare for a sales presentation so it is effective, ProActive, and really interesting to the prospect? Just follow the Muhammad Ali School of Presentations format.

The great Muhammad Ali adopted a theory of boxing he used late in his career. In the twilight of his boxing career he knew he was fighting men who were stronger, younger, and faster than he was, and if he went toe-to-toe with them in the boxing ring, his odds of winning were low. Aware that he was aging, he developed a school of thought that if his job was to win the fight, the most likely way he was going to win was not by a knockout but by a decision of the boxing judges. He believed that boxing judges were most impressionable in the first 30 seconds and the last 30 seconds of every round. In the middle of a round, he would save his strength, cover up, and do the rope-a-dope. (This is a boxing term Muhammad invented for a ploy whereby he would just lie on the ropes of the boxing ring and let his opponent punch him while he protected himself, letting his opponent get tired while he rested.) This gave him the strength for the last 30 seconds of the round to make a lasting impression on the judges.

Presentations are very similar. The opening and closing discussions of any presentation are the most important; they are the controlling parts of the sales meeting. The middle of the meeting, the product and service discussion, is the rope-a-dope. The beginning and end of a presentation are the tactical areas to focus on to maintain control. The middle is useful, and it contains the most information, but it's not how you gain and stay in control. You use the middle of the presentation to discuss what you are selling and to get input from the prospect. The middle of the presentation or sales education part of the sales call must be organized in a "Them, Then Us" format. This is very important from a prospect's standpoint because the sales presentation should be all about them. The format of the middle of the sales call/presentation needs to be:

1. Them
2. Us
3. Them

What Not to Do in the Middle

Don't use "Map Presentations."

A Map Presentation is one in which the salesperson delivers a presentation, usually in PowerPoint, to a room of prospects. The first slide is the title slide with the salesperson's company and logo information. The second and third slides are all about the company history and performance. At about the third or fourth slide, a picture of a map or globe comes up, and there are some stars or dots that highlight where the selling organization has offices or factories located around the world.

It is a very attractive slide and looks impressive (see Figure 7-1). But this kind of presentation is totally ineffective, since it's in an "Us–Them–Us" format.

And why on earth would the prospect care where your offices around the world are? So why would you put this map slide in the front of your presentation? Are you trying to impress the customer?

"I'm trying to establish credibility," you answer.

Stop and think. If you weren't credible, you wouldn't be in there giving a presentation. The only reason prospects, especially vice presidents, agree to a meeting is because they have a question to ask. They don't want to see a map with your locations on it. They want to talk—about

Figure 7-1 Map Presentation: Our Office Locations . . .

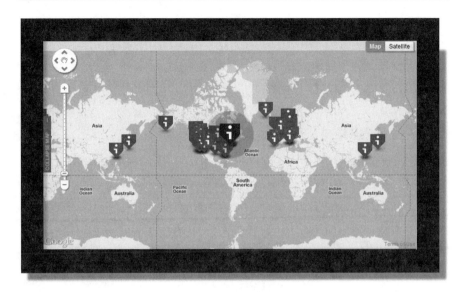

themselves. Remember: It's all about them.

What You Should Do in the Middle: Them–Us–Them

The middle of the presentation must focus on them, so start with talking about them, and end with talking about them. In the middle, you can talk about you—briefly. Have your first few slides of this middle part of the presentation be based on your homework or on leading questions to get them talking. You want at least the first 20 percent of the meeting to be about them. Your slides or presentation material should stimulate thought and get them involved.

Then there should be a natural lead into what you do and how they can apply what you do to the conversation you just had about them. No one wants to sit through a presentation and listen to what you have to say about you for longer than 5 or 10 minutes at a time. This goes back to the "buyer's value proposition" discussed in Chapter 1. No one cares about *your* value proposition. They care about *their own* value proposition—the value they are supplying to *their* customers—and how they can become more competitive. The middle of your presentation should reflect this interest.

End the middle part of the presentation with what the information about you means to them. Use Feature/Benefit and Feature/Benefit/ Value statements (see Chapter 2) to summarize your points, and then stimulate their thinking by asking questions about what this means to them or how they would use this.

Part 3: The Ending—The Mutual Agreement to a Next Step

Now it is time for the Ending. You've done a great job in getting the prospect involved in the beginning, getting their issues out on the table, and tailoring the middle of your presentation so they "get it." You've delivered your story and related it to the discussion you mutually had in the beginning. It's now time to end the presentation—in a way that keeps the sales process going.

The Ending is a way for you to summarize the meeting, gain agreement, and then offer a next step. In other words, you need to use the Summarize, Bridge, and Pull^{Tool} (see Chapter 5) to finish a presentation.

Your Ending can be very formal and last twenty minutes or so, based on the complexity of the issues or the risk involved in a next step, or it could take five minutes, based on the simplicity of moving forward. The Ending of a presentation follows three rules.

1. Follow the format of an SBP.
2. Keep prospects involved by having them do an SBP with your guidance.
3. Create a SalesMap.

To follow the format of an SBP, you should:

♦ Sum up the meeting (Summarize).
♦ Gain agreement (Bridge).
♦ Propose a next step (Pull).

Figure 7-2 shows the SBP process in a nutshell. During the Summarize part you should sum up what was discussed at the meeting, staying focused on the prospect's solution, not on what you are offering. A 3:1 ratio of what they've said they desire to what you are offering is a guideline for how much you should focus and talk about the prospect during the summary.

The Bridge is a way to get them to discuss the presentation itself, the

Figure 7-2 Follow the SBP

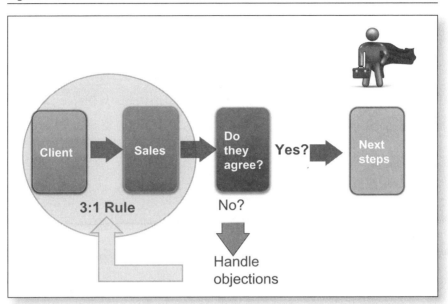

pros and the cons, and to have them air their true feelings about your presentation, as well as offer up any final objections.

Pulling to the next step includes the final summary and offering up the next step in the Buy/Sell process so that you stay in control of the meeting. The ending of the ProActive sales presentation must be interactive and have the prospect involved, so much so that it will feel like the prospects are closing themselves. If you do it right, they really are closing themselves, with you in control.

The Customer Pen: Keep Them Involved

Many salespeople close a meeting with a customer pen. They have a Magic Marker or "Customer Pen" they bring out at the end of a meeting. To keep the prospect involved, they give the pen to the top-ranking executive in the meeting and ask,

"Would you mind taking this pen, going to the board, and summarizing today's meeting so we can make sure we are all on the same page?"

What usually happens is that the executive gets up and goes to the board, or gives the pen to someone the executive trusts, and he or she goes to the board and starts to summarize the meeting. They start out slowly and usually need a little prompting, but after a minute or so they start to close themselves.

"... and if we had this system, we then could use it on that new project that just got stuck last week in engineering..."

The salesperson now transforms from being a musician in the orchestra during a concert to being the conductor, leading all the elements in one song rather than having different conversations and opinions going on at the same time and having to manage it all themselves.

So now we have the start, finish, and end to a great sales call.

There is an exception to steps in the Buyer's Buy/Sell process, however. Russians and Spaniards need to be treated differently. Here's what you need to know about senior management sales calls:

LAW OF SENIOR MANAGEMENT

Russians never want to be Educated, they want to be Validated!

This being the case, how you set up the Education sales call is important. You can use the same presentation to educate that you can use to validate. It's in how you set the call up. And, yes, there's a tool for that.

TOOL Ask 'em/Tell 'em/Ask 'em^{Tool}

Let's say you have an hour for a sales call. You would typically set it up like this:

Educate Call

5–10 minutes: Introduction (TELL 'em)
30–45 minutes: Middle (TELL 'em)
5–10 minutes: Summary (TELL 'em)

A classic way of education. Tell them what you're going to tell them, tell them, and then tell them what you've just told them. For a senior management meeting, however, you need to switch that up a bit. You need to have a validation meeting, not an educational meeting.

Validate Call

20–30 minutes: Questions (ASK 'em)
5–10 minutes: Middle (TELL 'em)
10–20 minutes: Summary, next steps (ASK 'em)

Education Call	Validation Call
• Tell them (what you are going to say)	• Ask them (what they want to discuss)
• Tell them	• Tell them (what you do and how it can help them)
• Tell them (what you have said)	• Ask them (what you both have said, agree, then SBP)

See the difference? The education way of sales presentations is very one-directional. You speak at the client, a Spaniard, and they listen: Tell 'em, tell 'em, and tell 'em. The classic, "I'm the person who is going to use what you are selling, so I need to know all about it."

The validation way gets the Business Case Buyer, the Russian, involved up front, since the reason they are there is to validate the process and the choice. They don't care how it works; they only care *that* it works, and that it will bring them the savings or revenue they need. The validation call creates more mutual involvement and is under your control, and therefore you have more control over the outcome of the meeting. Validation sales presentations go like this:

1. The salesperson—you—starts out in control of the meeting and involves the prospect by asking him what he wants to accomplish.

2. You then inform the prospect of what you do and how it relates to their needs (which you got him to tell you about at the beginning of the meeting). You both talk about WIIFM.

3. You finish the presentation with a SBP and ask (pull) the prospect if he wants to go to a next step.

It's a simple, clean, and winning formula.

Now, go and change those slides. Give a ProActive sales presentation, and educate or validate your prospect in a ProActive manner.

A Few Final Tips on Sales Presentations

1. Get rid of map presentations or map slides. No one cares where your home office is.

2. Use Magic Markers, lots of Magic Markers. These are probably the most powerful sales education tools you can find. ProActive salespeople always carry a set of multicolored magic markers in their briefcases. How many times have you tried to make your sales presentation in a meeting room with an old, semi-dried-out green Magic Marker? Not very visually appealing or convincing. Use color, and a lot of it. It will keep your presentation in the prospect's mind longer, and make a competitive difference, since most reactive salespeople are using that old green marker.

3. Write down the benefits of every feature you want to reinforce. (In color!) Don't just write down the feature, write down the benefit and its value to the prospect (FBV). Remember, WIIFM is the major theme.

4. Use multiple media. A flip chart and a projector are more powerful than just using a projector. If you are only going to use a flip chart, use two! Write a feature (and its benefit) on a single page; then do the same for a second feature/benefit. Reference the first whenever appropriate during the meeting, moving their attention back and forth.

5. Keep the energy going. Ask questions and get them involved. Ask *"What would you do with . . ."* questions to keep them involved. Don't make them listen to you speak for longer than 5 or 10 minutes at a time. The brain can only take so much one-way communication before it shuts down. You may be having a great time and be really on a roll making a great point, but if the members of your audience have turned off their brains, nothing will get through. Stick with that 5-to-10-minute rule.

6. Use anecdotes. Stories are great education tools. When you are making a point, use a story. It becomes a powerful anchor.

7. Have them write something down. Give them a quiz. Ask for their opinions. Give them a simple worksheet to fill out. In the middle of the presentation, a way of getting them involved is having them write something down, even if it is to write what they have just heard you say down on a post-it note. Having them write something down helps them to remember, and the act of writing it down is a great way for objections to come out and for you to get them to share what is on their mind.

It's All About ME!

The prospect must be thought of in the introduction, in the middle, and at the end of a sales presentation, period. Practice by having some other salespeople and non-salespeople sit in and critique your next presentation. Have some office administrators sit in as well, and ask them all to tell you what they have heard. If they start to repeat all the things you have said about your offering, or even if they just keep the focus of the discussions on your product/features, you've done it wrong. If they start to state what they've heard and what it means to them, how they're going to use it, you've done it right.

It's hard to keep the focus of the conversation on them. There usually comes a time when the prospect wants to hear more, or a panic time when you're at a loss to answer a direct question the prospect is asking. The natural tendency is to go back to what you know best: product knowledge. This is the last thing you should do.

Practice, Practice, Practice

Practice reference stories, practice asking other secondary questions, and practice Flips until you are as comfortable with these as you are with the product features. ProActive selling is about having comebacks and Flips to move managers who want to keep the presentation at the Feature/ Function (Spanish) level to the Benefit and Value (Russian) level. ProActive selling is certainly not about being the salesperson who has the most product knowledge and speaks the most fluent Spanish. Practice these tactics to get good at them. Winging it, or just saying whatever comes to your mind at the time, is a reactive and risky technique at best.

The best question that works at all three levels and makes sure you are focusing on the prospect during sales education is the "so what" question.

"So what does that mean to you?"
"So what would you do with this?"

"So what else will you be doing when this is implemented?"
"So what would stop you from going ahead with this?"
"So what . . . ?"

The "So what . . . ?" question is what the other people in the practice session should be asking you, and you should be asking yourself on every point you make. This ensures you have the prospect's best interest in mind and are ready for any objections.

Be ProActive, and learn how to get comfortable talking about *them*. They want to talk about themselves, and you should let them; you'll sell more if you do.

The Danger in the Unspoken Feature

Here is a word of caution for ProActive salespeople: Salespeople, like everyone else, get bored saying the same thing over and over. What's worse, they assume that since they have said it for the last 200 meetings they have been in, that everyone knows it, and therefore it's a commodity. The unspoken feature ends up being your competitor's exclusive.

Too many deals have been lost by the prospect saying, *"I didn't know you offered that as well,"* or the salesperson saying, *"I told them that when we first met. It's not my fault they didn't remember."* Yes, it *is* your fault.

There are hundreds of reasons why prospects should buy your product/service, but they end up focusing on just two or three, and usually it's a different two or three for every buyer. When you find what prospects want, you should repeat the feature you have that meets their need, and the benefit and the value it provides, over and over again. You have won deals because the prospect liked a key feature you offer and the benefits it provided. Your competitor has that same feature/benefit, something similar, or another feature/benefit that you do not have. Find out what is important to prospects, and then tell them over and over again. Get them to tell you over and over. Someone is talking about the unspoken feature, and it is usually that someone who gets the order.

The Right Order

You have an important sales call next Wednesday, and you want to be prepared. How should you prepare? You know that every sales call has a beginning (30-Second Speech, no question), a middle (*hmmm*, Features/Benefits/Values followed by customer-led discussion?), and an end (SBP, without a doubt). *"Should I start at the beginning and work my way through? Seems logical, no?"*

Well, no, that's exactly the wrong way to go about it.

It's really very simple: All great sales calls start *with the end in mind.* So the first element you work on is the end. Before you even think about what you want to have happen during the sales call, you must think,

> "If this call goes well, what is the next step I want to have happen? What is my best outcome and next step? What do I want them to do when this meeting is over?"

You first need to construct your SBP. If this is a first call, you do not know the *You/I* part of the SBP, but your goal will be to listen for these so you can stay in control as the meeting comes to a close. Since you know the steps of the buying process, you should usually be aiming for the next step in the buy process. If you are at Educate, pull to Validate; if at Validate, go on to Justify; and so on.

If you start with the end in mind, your next question is, *"How do I want to introduce the call?"* or *"How should I start the call, now that I know how I want it to end?"* When you plan Step 3 first, then Step 1, you usually change what you were going to say in Step 2. So the right order to plan for a sales call is:

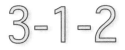

Go ahead try it. Plan your sales calls with the end in mind. Start with the SBP, then the 30-Second Speech. When you have those two elements, you'll be able to design the content of what you want to say around the beginning and the end, so to give you control of the total sales call, not just the middle.

Ending a sales call in control is just as important as how you start the call, probably even more. If your goal is to stay in control in the early process of the Buy/Sell cycle, these ending tools are critical for your success.

Now armed with the right order, there are two tools you can use to keep the prospects involved and keep the conversation focused on their needs: GAP Charts and SalesMaps.

TOOL | **GAP Chart**^{Tool}

A GAP Chart is a tool you can use to keep the meeting focused on the prospect, to find their trains, and to quantify their problems and your value all at the same time (see Figure 7-3). (Remember "Leveraging Trains" from Chapter 3? Useful concept, isn't it?)

In business, there is usually either a positive or negative gap related to a fixed goal—that is, a company expects to exceed its objectives or, on the contrary, not reach them. For example, imagine a prospect with a $10M goal for the year for a new product launch. If you ask, six months into the goal, how they are doing, you would hear one of three options:

1. *"Great, everything looking good. There is actually some potential upside."*

2. *"Good. We are right on track."*

3. *"It's going to be tight. I think we are close, but we're probably looking at a deficit."*

The executive who states option 2, *"We are right on track,"* will not want to talk about this issue, since it's doing fine and needs little attention. What you are looking for is the executive who is thinking "upside" or "deficit." Why? Because they are looking for answers they do not have. They need help closing the gap.

Figure 7-3 GAP Chart^{Tool}

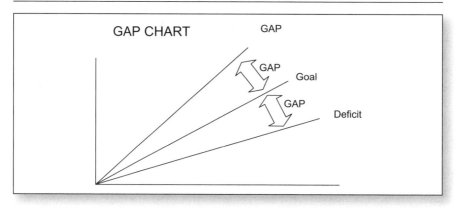

Prospects want to solve their problems, and if you can help them solve their problems, they're going to give you and your proposal special consideration—especially since all your other competitors are probably just pitching products and hoping something sticks.

For example, you have a meeting with a VP, a dyed-in-the-wool Russian, complete with wolves, borscht, and vodka (lots of vodka!) and you're nervous. You've got two choices.

1. Tell him who you are, what you are doing with the managers you've been meeting with, and hope he sees value in what you are doing.

2. Ask him about problems she's facing over the next six to nine months, listen for gaps, show how you can help to close the gaps, and create value. This effort rarely involves any discussion of the features you've been discussing in the meetings you've been having.

Russians don't have their issues or ideas fully resolved yet, and need help to close the gap. Let's look at a typical situation.

Imagine the C-level marketing executive, John, sitting in his office at the end of the quarter. There are some trains he is working on, and he needs his trains to be completed to address his goals, objectives, commitments, and his paycheck.

He's reviewing his annual objectives right before your meeting. He notices a few that are looking good, and a few that need work. He'll have to come up with some ideas

In your meeting with John, you ask him what is the one thing right now that he feels he's at the most risk for the next six to nine months. He might tell you,

"It's the new product rollout. I have committed a $10M revenue figure for the first nine months, and it looks like it's going to be short."

So you ask, *"How short do you think?"* John answers, *"About 20 percent."* There you have your gap.

Next, ask John what he's doing to close the gap (see Figure 7-4). Usually, executives have something they're working on (they aren't clueless), and he will usually come up with a few things he's got in process. These would be active trains.

Figure 7-4 John's GAP Chart

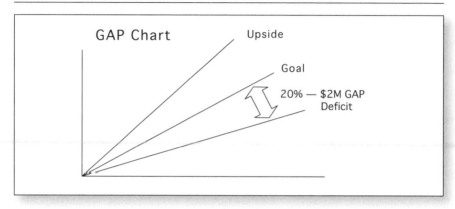

"Well, I'm working on getting more channels involved, adding a separate product addition to pull the sales through, and offering the sales team added commission to really get their attention."

You need to qualify these three trains. *"Can you put some numbers to these plans?"* you ask.

"Sure. I need three more channels on board in the next sixty days, I need that product to have a $5,000 selling price to attract the new market, and I think with added commission, I can get 20 percent more from the current sales team. I don't have the details worked out yet, however."

"So, Mr. Smith, if you could have these three issues resolved in the next two months, what would that do to the $2M you need?"

"Well, I can see at least $1.5 to 2M in these three areas alone."

"We at XYZ Company can help you get there."

You have now done a few things:

1. You have identified the prospect's crucial priorities, the issues for which they have no answers yet.
2. You have persuaded the prospect to assign a value to these issues.
3. You have said that you can help achieve that value. You are not the entire answer, but you *are* a part of the answer.

4. If your product/service costs, say, $100K, the VP is going to weigh the $100K investment to the overall $2M. At this point, do you really think he cares if you are $100 or $120K?

You are at a competitive advantage. Your competitor has not shown that he will help John achieve that value.

You can always be ProActive and suggest items into the conversation in question form if the prospect is not covering an area that you offer.

"Those are good items, Mr. Smith. Have you also considered new packaging schemes or appealing to a different buyer?"

Since these are areas with which you can help, you probably want to bring them up so you can judge if it's an area they would even consider (disqualification; more about that in Chapter 10).

A GAP Chart is a great tool to be used with a Russian. It rarely works with a Spaniard, since they are only doing what they have been told to do; they don't have control over the options as Russians do. The GAP Chart quantifies value and attacks the area of most concern to the executive-level buyer, the Russian.

Road Map to the Deal

You and the prospect now have enough information from using the tactics you have just mastered during the sales education phase of selling. It is now time to finish the sales education phase, Summarize, Bridge, and Pull to the next step called Validate. Before doing that, however, you need one more tool, the SalesMap^{Tool}.

TOOL SalesMap^{Tool}

Most salespeople, at the end of the Educate step, feel confident about their chances. It is now that the deal can either be solidly entrenched in your camp, or can slip though your fingers. Salespeople often ask,

"How can I as a salesperson lead the prospect through the rest of the sale rather than feel like I am being led and being reactive? Is there a way to map out the rest of the Buy/Sell cycle and stay in control from this point forward?"

There is in fact a map that identifies the steps that need to be taken by both prospect and seller, and how to have the prospect and seller agree on these steps while the salesperson stays in control. It's like an SBP but describes the rest of the Buy/Sell process to the prospect. It then allows the salesperson to take control of the rest of the process, not just a single step. It's called the SalesMap.

Before we get to the SalesMap tool (aha, anticipation should heighten your interest!), let me tell you a personal story.

I was born and raised in Cleveland, Ohio. Every December, we would travel to Tampa, Florida, for the holidays. All eight of us would get into the car, complain about who was sitting where, and head to Tampa.

Once on the road, the only people who knew where we were going were my mom, my dad, and the AAA (American Automobile Association). Why? Because every year my parents would get a series of maps from the AAA called a Trip-Tik. This Trip-Tik was a series of maps bound in a book that was customized for the member who was taking a trip by car. For us, our Trip-Tik would start in Cleveland, and at the bottom of the first page, would end in Columbus, Ohio. If you turned the page, it would then start at Columbus, and at the bottom of the second page would be Cincinnati. There were twenty to twenty-five pages in all, and it would finally end with the bottom of the last page in Tampa. This was great. Page one had CLEVELAND to COLUMBUS; at the last page, you were SOMEWHERE IN FLORIDA NEAR TAMPA to TAMPA. In between were all the roads and exits we had to take to get to Tampa. It highlighted the detours, hotels, restaurants, and even places where speed traps might have been set up by the state highway patrols. It basically detailed the route we should take to get to Tampa, and what we could expect along the way.

What a fabulous tool! If we didn't have a Trip-Tik we could all have piled in the car, started in Cleveland, and ended up in Houston—which is certainly a great place, but not where we wanted to go.

The Trip-Tik was a mutual guide for us getting to our destination. We decided where we wanted to go, worked with our partners, who told us how to get there, and followed their directions. The *Pro-Active Selling* SalesMap is a mutual guide for prospects to get to their destination, which is a choice. Prospects decide where they want to go, usually work with a single partner who is in control of the sale, and follow the sales team's directions because they have confidence in their ability and professionalism based on the completeness of a SalesMap.

These are two different journeys, but use the same effective tool.

Figure 7-5 SalesMap

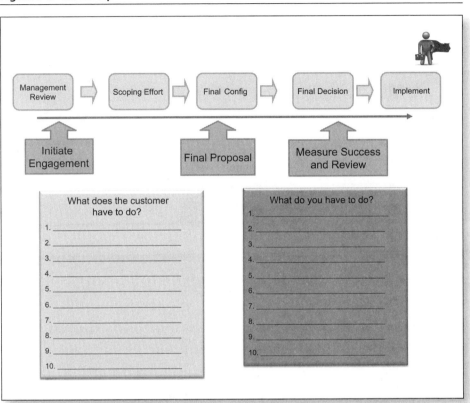

Figure 7-5 is an example of a SalesMap. A SalesMap should be a document that is mutually worked on in the beginning, then referenced and updated at every opportunity.

Here's what your working document might look like (see Figure 7-6): Insert steps the prospect is going to be taking on their own.

Update this SalesMap after every sales call!

The SalesMap is one of two tools discussed in *ProActive Selling* that everyone agrees has a tremendous amount of value, but it takes some work to develop and implement. (The other, The Implementation Plan-Tool—equally valuable, and equally underutilized—is discussed in Chapter 11.) Many salespeople agree with the idea of a SalesMap, but fail to implement it since it requires some planning and some effort to get good at. If you really want to control the sales process, you must use the tools, especially the SalesMap. It's the best way to control the sales process, be-

Figure 7-6 Sample SalesMap

Prospect Company: _____

Contact Name: _____

Initial Sales Call Date: _____ / _____ / _____

What are the steps we have taken together so far?

1. _____

2. _____

3. _____

What are the next buy/sell steps you want to take to make sure a decision is made?

	Complete?	
	Yes	No
1. _____	☐	☐
2. _____	☐	☐
3. _____	☐	☐
4. _____	☐	☐
5. _____	☐	☐

Insert steps the prospect is going to be taking on their own.

---

cause it requires mutual collaboration. It's tough to build a house without a blueprint; it's tougher to win a sale without a SalesMap. Additionally, some general SalesMap rules are:

♦ You should have more items about them on the SalesMap than your items. It's all about them, not about all the stuff you are going to do for them.

♦ If the prospect does not want to work with you on developing a SalesMap, it may be a disqualifying action.

♦ You can have a Russian SalesMap and a Spanish SalesMap.

- You never present a SalesMap. It's something the prospect must participate in and with. If they don't want to work with you on something that is all about them, see "disqualifying action" two bullets up.

- Eventually, a SalesMap goes past the decision date and starts getting to implementation. All the better.

- Make sure their logo is bigger than your logo. It's all about them.

You're on a roll. You've completed what has to be done in the Educate process to feel confident and really understand what prospects want. They understand what you do and the value they will get by buying from you, and you have covered all the bases. It's looking very good.

But wait! There's still more to teach you about the Educate step. Education is a two-way street! Read all about it in the next chapter.

CHAPTER 8

Educate the Customer Using Two-Way Learning

SALESPEOPLE AND SALES MANAGERS have varied viewpoints on what sales education is. Here's what sales education is *not*:

◆ Telling the prospect all about yourself.

◆ Telling the prospect the features of your product/service. This would be a regurgitation of product knowledge—something every salesperson wants to do, but really needs to do less.

◆ Spewing out a standard sales presentation.

◆ A demonstration of a product or service.

◆ A one-way conversation about your product/service and what it can do for the customer.

◆ A proposal.

◆ Marketing literature delivered in e-mail, on the Web, in mail, or in person.

◆ A contract.

Here's what ProActive sales education *is*:

THE LAW OF PROACTIVE SALES EDUCATION

Sales education is where you find out the real needs and motivation of the prospective customer, you determine *with the prospect* whether there is a mutual fit, and then you go on to determine, again *with the prospect*, why the customer should make a decision to change.

Let's look at this in three parts:

1. *Find out the real needs and motivation of the prospective customer.* This *must* be done first. The philosophy of the salesperson or sales team must be to find out what is really driving a need, and to identify the real motivation behind this need. What are their real issues? (So, we might wonder, why are so many slide presentations reactive, starting off with facts and figures about your company and its products/services, rather than probing the prospect?)

2. *Determine whether there is a mutual fit.* The goal of sales education is not to convince someone to buy something from you; that would be a very one-dimensional approach. The real purpose of sales education is for the seller and the buyer mutually to agree on doing something. (This means that you must know about the buyer's needs and motivation before you can start to educate the prospective buyer on the features and benefits of what you are offering. You must do your homework!)

3. *Determine with the prospect why he or she should make a decision to change.* The purpose is to have the customer determine with the salesperson (together, so that there is a transfer of ownership) whether the prospect should make a decision for change.

   The ProActive salesperson understands that a salesperson is trying to sell something. Buyers, however, are not really buying something; they are *changing* something. They want or need to change. Most people don't like to change. They will make a purchase, do something different, reengineer, or develop something to invoke this needed change. You're hoping they'll make a purchase, and that they'll purchase your product/service to satisfy this need for change. Great, but don't lose sight of the buyer's perspective. Selling them something is very one-dimensional. They want or need to change, and what you must offer is a vehicle to assist or satisfy their need. This should be a mutual win-win transaction.

The bottom line is that you are not selling something to someone. Think like a buyer, be ProActive, and understand his or her need for change. Help them with it, and create a mutual win-win. For successful salespeople this definition of sales education is second nature.

Creating Value Early

An additional requirement for the salesperson is to assist the buyer in creating value for the solution/service/product that is being offered. Remember, value is in the buyer's mind, not necessarily the seller's.

What is value? What is not value? Why must it be established early? These are some great questions that need to be looked at if the salesperson's job of mutual education is to be accomplished.

What is value? In the business world, value is anything that can make something more efficient, solve a problem, or save or make money. It is all about buyers' motivations for change, and how they value the change of whatever they are doing to themselves and the company. Value can be defined in business goals, such as saving cost, or in personal goals, such as getting a business promotion.

What is not *value?* Value has very little to do with your product or service on a stand-alone basis. Prospects don't value you, or what your products/service can do. They do value what you or your products/service can do for *them*.

There are two goals in establishing value.

1. It has to be early in the process.
2. It has to be quantified.

Without a mutually agreed-upon value defined early in the process, both the buyer and seller will get caught up in the following two situations that will doom a deal to a pricing game.

♦ They both will focus on the features of what the seller is selling. Both parties will evaluate, conduct a demonstration, compare features to the competition, and generally get lost in feature-based needs. The value that comes out of this war is who is a better fit, but in no way determines the winner.

♦ Upon winning or coming close in the needs war, the selling team will, near the end of the process, request a meeting with the more senior management of the company to go over the needs of the customer, and how they are uniquely qualified to meet those needs.

Both these discussions focus on the wrong value proposition. They are focusing on what the product/service can do—its features. The value of a product or service is not its features, but how it can specifically resolve the *reason* the prospect is making a change in the first place.

To avoid the distraction of the features/benefit focus, the value—in terms of the prospect's needs—must be quantified early in the process. Get the prospect to put an amount on what a solution can bring to their organization. It can be a dollar amount, a time amount, any unit of measure that is important to them. This is a great disqualifying step, to see if the prospect is just kicking tires or if there is a real business need. (More about disqualifying in Chapter 10.) Understanding the prospect's motivation and quantifying it early in the process will tell you if the prospect has a specific value defined—and therefore the motivation needed to complete the Buy/Sell process. Without a defined value, the sales process will slowly lose steam, and "fighting for budget dollars," "looking at it again," and "trying to find a good time for us to go forward" will become the norm.

Getting Their Attention

So what should the goal of a salesperson be early in the Buy/Sell process? Simply put, the goals are to uncover the business motivation and the needs of the User Buyer, which takes you right back to "cause" and "effect"—the two approaches based on User Buyers and Business Case Buyers, discussed at length in Chapter 2.

Thus, the real goal of sales education is twofold:

1. Educate the User Buyer to understand that you can respond to their list of needs and requirements.

2. Educate the Business Case Buyer to understand that you can respond with your products or services to whatever is causing them to change, to do something different—that is, that you

will help enable the Business Case Buyer to reach their overall business goals.

In reality, as explained in Chapter 2, there are two sales occurring simultaneously, and the appropriate value for each type of buyer needs to be extracted out of each sale.

Selling Solutions and Finding Trains

As customer problems become much more complex, salespeople are being required to sell much more complex answers. Selling point solutions is still an acceptable selling methodology, but customers expect more sophisticated solutions to their intricate problems from their vendors.

What is selling or providing solutions anyway? With so many perspectives and definitions, it may be beneficial to describe selling from both the salesperson and customer viewpoints. We have a tool, the Solution Box^{Tool}, that can help you figure out how your product/service can help solve the Russian's larger problems (see Figure 8-1).

TOOL | Solution Box^{Tool}

If you look at what you are selling as multiple pieces in a puzzle, you can craft a solution by pulling together various pieces of the puzzle. Think of a User Buyer who has a need. We'll call this need an empty box. They need the box full so they can resolve their problem and meet their needs. Your job is to fill the box, and offer the most complete solution you can. We'll call that Solution Box A.

As you can see, Box A has been almost completely filled by your solution. You have worked very hard at matching your User Buyer's needs to what you have to offer. You put together some of Product A, a bit of Product B, a few line items from some other products, and then added a bit of packaging magic, a small discount, and a bit faster delivery than usual, and voila, you have a complete Solution Box A.

But there's a small problem. While your Solution Box A is a fine offering, and will be considered along with a host of other solutions the prospect is considering, there is another solution box the prospect is working on. Welcome to Solution Box B.

Solution Box B is the Business Case Buyer's box. Business Case Buyers have a problem as well that needs attention—and there are many pieces needed to fill this Solution Box. Unlike with Solution Box A,

Figure 8-1 Solution Box^{Tool}

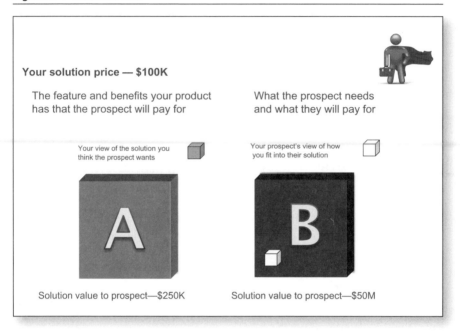

however, for Solution Box B you are only one piece of the solution, not the entire solution.

The problem that Solution Box B needs to resolve is a much bigger issue than the product or service you are selling. For Solution Box A, value was defined by how much you could fill up the box with a solution. For Solution Box B, value is defined by how well you fit with all the other pieces in the box. As a result, you are required to understand the other pieces of Solution Box B, and demonstrate how what you offer fits into Solution Box B, and works well with those other pieces.

To demonstrate the difference between the two Solution Boxes, here is the Solution Box "Which Box" Quiz.

Which Box?

For each case outlined below, determine which Solution Box is most appropriate.

1. The salesperson sits down with the prospect and listens to what they really need—that is, what specific things they are

looking for the solution to accomplish. The salesperson, after listening to these needs, tells the prospect what they do, and how it fits their needs perfectly. Which Box?

2. The salesperson gets a list of requirements (RFP, RFQ), and is to respond to these lists by offering their solution to the list. Which Box?

3. The prospect wants to see the item you are offering in operation, or talk to a current user of that item. After all, they are the ones who are going to have to make it work and live with it daily. Which Box?

4. The prospect has defined a $5M effort in which they are currently engaged, and the need to get a return on this investment. They have explained that they see you and your company as an enabling piece to help get them this return. Which Box?

5. The prospect wants to go over the proposal line by line and make sure they are getting what they need for the money they are spending. Which Box?

6. The meeting was an hour, and all you did was ask questions about business goals and challenges in the future. The prospect described major initiatives and challenges that were on their company's plate for the next 6 to 12 months, and how they need help with those issues. Which Box?

7. The budget for the decision is $40,000. Your proposal is $47,000. The prospect has told you that your solution is a great fit and they love your proposal, but they only have a maximum of $40,000 to spend. Which Box?

8. The solution the company is looking for is an $8M investment. You solution fits into what they have defined as their overall objective, and costs $47,000. Which Box?

The answers are Solution Box A: 1, 2, 3, 5, and 7; Solution Box B: 4, 6, and 8.

Without understanding the two different types of Solution Boxes, most salespeople will only address Solution Box A, including discounting to match what the prospect has defined as his or her value in terms of a budget. Having worked very hard to put Solution Box A together, salespeople are intently focused on explaining the features and benefits of Solution Box A.

ProActive salespeople will also go hunting early for Solution Box B. The Business Case Buyer will describe an overriding initiative/challenge/investment they are making in a Solution Box B format, and then will also tell you what it's worth. You may hear comments like these:

> *"This is worth $50M to us in the next twelve months, so investing between $5 and $7M in this still gives us a great return. If your product can do what you say it can, and is going to cost us about $40 or $50,000, this may be a good fit."*

> *"Our goal next year is $70M for this new product. I see us getting to $50M, but we need some help getting the other $20M."*

> *"I see where you are coming from. This will allow us some flexibility in what we are doing next year, and to get to the $7M goal we need to get to. How much is what you are selling again? $47,000?"*

We first introduced the concept of "trains" in Chapter 3, where we compared the typical vice president (Russian) you work with to a station manager, who has many trains (projects) under his or her watch. We showed how you could leverage value across projects. This is the tool you will use to help you do just that.

TOOL | Finding Trains^{Tool}

A further complication to the Solution Box B sale is that senior executives often have multiple Solution Box Bs on which they are working. Too often, salespeople find a Solution Box B, get excited, and want to close a deal. Hold on. If you look at what is really going on in the life of a C-level executive, you'll notice that they are dealing with more than one issue at a time—more than one Solution Box B at a time. To put all this in perspective, we offer the Finding Trains^{Tool}.

Think of the Business Case Buyer as a train station master, the person who is in charge of the train station.

Their job is to make sure the trains get out on time without any problems. A station master can be any C-level executive, since each one has his or her own trains. For instance, an example of some trains for a VP of marketing would be:

- Get two new products launched by the end of the first quarter.
- Examine new markets and report to executive board by the first of the month.
- Get trade show materials ready and committed by the end of next month.
- Organize and prepare executive road show to top EMEA customers by the end of the year.
- Create and approve new marketing materials before the next sales meeting.
- Select new lead generation and marketing collaboration system by the end of next quarter.

The list can go on and on, and which of these "trains" is important to the VP depends on the situation. Let's assume that the VP currently has five "trains" or Solution Box Bs on his desk (see Figure 8-2).

Figure 8-2 A Busy Station Master (Russian)

The five trains are all current topics and goals on which he and his team are working. You have a meeting with the station master, and you find out that each train has to get out on time. Each train has a commitment and other trains are due in the station. VPs and station masters live in a stressful and complicated world.

You have a meeting with the VP/station master, and find out the following status:

- ◆ Train 1: Looking good. Missing a few first-class dinners and a few passengers, but looking good to get out on time.
- ◆ Train 2: Real problem. Missing some first-class cars and about 20 passengers. Has to leave the train station in 45 minutes.
- ◆ Train 3: OK. Missing some food, some cargo, but all in all, OK. Could be a candidate for improvement though.
- ◆ Train 4: Big problem. Not even in the train station yet, and it's got an important run it has to make on its next trip.
- ◆ Train 5: Some issues. Could use a new conductor, some new seats, and needs an overhaul if the ROI is good enough.

To complete the metaphor, you find out that you can help the station master on trains 2, 3, and 5. As a result, you will be talking to the VP for some time to come, you'll develop a partnership rather than a vendor relationship, and you'll be creating value for the VP in many different ways beyond just selling a product. Value to a station master is created across trains, not focused on one train only.

Train Station Rules

1. Every C-level executive has multiple trains in their train station, and the trains are always changing based on when they get completed or when they get reassigned.

2. Trains differ in their importance.

3. You can get access to the station master in different ways. Don't get locked into one way.

4. Station masters don't want to talk about your products/services . . . yet. They are paying their conductors to solve those problems.

5. Instead, they want to talk about their trains . . . to anyone who will listen.

6. Station masters with the same titles all seem to have similar trains.

There are multiple examples of how the "trains" scenario can play out. For example, the conductor of Train 1 may have brought you in, and as a result you get to spend some time with the station manager. As explained in Chapter 3, your goal would not only be to confirm that you can help solve problems on Train 1, but also to ask about other trains that may have caused problems for the station manager over the last six months (past), or trains that may have trouble making their scheduled departure (future).

Your goal is to find an opportunity to leverage your company solutions across multiple trains (Solution Box Bs), not just to reaffirm what you are doing with Train 1. Remember when you are hunting for trains with the station master, that if you can offer to help with two to three trains, you will hit the jackpot—every time!

Another example could involve a meeting with the station master, during which he recognizes that you can help him with Train 2.

> "That's a really good solution you have there, and Jill, my conductor on Train 2, could really use it. Why don't you call on her?"

Armed with that referral, you are ready to dash out of the meeting and call Jill. What could be better than a meeting that Jill's boss has recommended?

Don't be in too much of a hurry. If you go right to Jill, the station master will think that you and your company can only solve the problems that exist on Train 2. This mindset on the part of the customer will most likely prevent you from eventually going broad and deep in this account. (*"Really, HP offers more than printers? I had no idea, and the salesperson never brought it up."*).

If the station master does bring up a train that they need help on, you should acknowledge the station master's opinion, saying thank you and that you will look into it. Then ask that great station master question:

> "Is there anything else?"

Remember, your goal is to find multiple trains with which you can help if possible—not to find one train and like a shark with blood in the water, jump on that one offer.

It's true that there will be many opportunities in which there is only one train in the train station with which you can help at the given time, or ever. Nevertheless, you always want to be asking for additional trains. Opportunities will come your way only if you ask, rather than "hanging out" at the train station hoping the station master will just happen to stroll by and ask you for something.

ProActive salespeople get good at asking for trains. This leads to more leverage, more opportunity, and more sales!

Now, let's go on to Chapter 9 and develop the skills you need to qualify—and *dis*qualify—your prospect.

Qualify: Not a Phase but a Process

YOU ARE NOW IN CONTROL of your sale. You started off doing homework on the accounts you wanted to call on. You know where you should be spending your time, what information you should be gathering, when you should be prospecting your A-level customers, and you know what to say in your sales opening to capture their interest. You then have implemented some sales education tools to make sure the prospect really understands WIIFM. You have actually developed a SalesMap with the prospect, and he or she has agreed to work with you on it. You already have ideas on where to spend your commission from this deal, since you know you have a highly qualified deal, right? Let's find out.

Qualification and Disqualification Skills

We need to define qualification and disqualification skills and tactics. Simply put:

Qualification skills are skills needed to continue to go forward in a sales process. You will qualify a company or someone in a company because that company or person is a "good fit account," has an interest, and has access to funds; therefore, the sales effort should continue.

There is typically a list of qualifying questions that need to be addressed to fully qualify a prospect as someone worth investing precious time and effort.

Disqualification skills are skills needed to learn how to stop a sales process. For example, you should disqualify a prospect who won't co-operate, but expects you to do all the work and then present them with a final quote or proposal. A good prospect is someone who will let you guide them through a Buy/Sell process and do their fair share in that process (see Figure 9-1). They will put an equal amount of "sweat equity" into a buy decision.

In this chapter, qualification skills will be addressed. Disqualification skills are discussed in Chapter 10 under "Homework Assignments."

How You Should Spend Your Time

In Chapter 1, the phases of the Buy/Sell process were outlined, as well as the way in which a ProActive salesperson goes through these phases step by step to win a deal. You have already made it through the generating in-

Figure 9-1 Buy/Sell Process: Qualifying

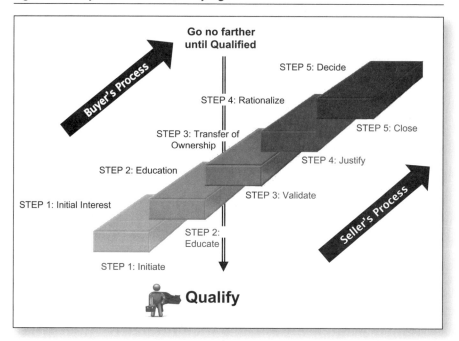

terest phase (Initiate), have finished up the Education step (Educate), and are heading for the Validation phase (Validate). Before you go any further in this sale, you have to make sure you have a qualified deal.

This is of course speaking from a salesperson's point of view. Salespeople and sales managers ask all the time,

"How can I make sure I really have a qualified situation?"

The answer is you can never be sure. You will, however, be given some tools right now to make sure you can confidently and effectively qualify a prospect.

Qualifying Goals

The goal of qualifying is to give you a better than 50 percent chance of closing the sale. That is all qualification skills should do. By making sure you are working a qualified deal you will:

- Work on the deals you have a better than 50 percent chance of winning, so you can increase your close ratio.
- Close more deals by eliminating the maybes.
- Force prospects into a decision as to whether they really want to continue with this Buy/Sell evaluation at this time.
- Stop working the 0 to 50 percent probability deals. Why would you work on these deals anyway? You have a better chance of winning in Las Vegas than trying to close a deal at 30 percent probability.
- Increase the chances for success early in the deal. You have not expended too many resources on this deal yet, but now it is ramping up, and you will be spending time and energy with demonstrations, proposals, and the like. The better you qualify early in the process, the sooner you can make a decision if this is a deal you want to be spending time on.

It may be hard to believe, but it's better to get rid of unqualified deals and get out there and prospect (not an unpleasant word anymore now that you have your ProActive tools). Getting rid of unqualified deals and prospecting some new opportunities makes good selling sense.

MMM: The Qualification Process

The *ProActive Selling* qualification process focuses on getting the qualification information from the prospect. To get information, you have to ask questions. To get good qualification information, you have to ask good questions.

Good qualification questions are centered on three probing areas, which are called the three Ms:

♦ Money

♦ Method

♦ Motivation

Qualification of a deal is a skill, and if it is mastered, it will affect your success more than anything else. In the years that *ProActive Selling* has been around, we've found that if a salesperson masters the MMM qualification questions, these questions will do more to affect a salesperson's income than anything else you learn in *ProActive Selling*. MMM has seven questions.

The Seven Questions

Did you ever wonder how you get to master great sales questions? You read books, watch sales videos, listen to sales training tapes, observe other top salespeople, and you try to pick up tips that will help you to sell more effectively. You know you have to ask great questions, but what are great questions? Great questions always seem to be on the sales training videotape, not in real life. In real life, you ask a question like:

"Do you have a budget for this project?"

In the sales training videotape, you hear the same question you are asking, but it comes out a little different.

"Mr. Lewis, given the benefits of the solution we are looking at, what would the process of obtaining budgetary funds be in your organization?"

Although this may seem like the same question, it isn't really. The seven qualifying questions will give you the ammunition you need to ask great qualification questions, starting with the first M, Money.

Money

Question #1: Money—What, Not Who

The first of our seven questions that we need to address concerns Money; this is the number one question to be answered. If the prospect doesn't have a way to pay for what you're offering, why would you be working on a particular deal? The prospect, without money or resources, may have you occupied for months and prevent you from working on sales opportunities with real potential.

There is one question for Money, but it is in two parts. First, however, every salesperson knows the real question he or she would like to ask concerning Money. All salespeople would love to look at the buyers they are talking to, especially Spanish ones, and point-blank ask:

> "Ms. Larsen, are you an important person in this process, or do I have to go over your head to get a decision?"

You cannot ask this question, but don't you wish you really could? This question is the wrong question because it focuses in the wrong place. It asks *who*, which is a big mistake. As a ProActive salesperson, you need to be asking *what*. The two parts of the *what* question you need to ask under Money are:

♦ "What is the process for obtaining a budget for a decision like this?"
♦ "What is the process for making a decision?"

These are the questions you ask under Money. Money focuses on the "what" questions. You want to focus on the *what* questions because "what" is a buyer's question—buyers ask themselves "what" all the time.

"What should we do from here?"

"What is the process we need to go through to get Jack to sign off on this project?"

"What do you think we should do first?"

"What approvals do you think we are going to need to get this project approved?"

"What do we have to do to get more money if we exceed the current budget?"

What questions are the questions the buyers are asking themselves all day long. After your sales manager has drilled you on "Who is making the decision?" you go in to the prospect and ask a sales question like your boss has told you to do:

"Who is buying our product/service?"
"Who has the budget?"
"Who is the person making the decision?"

The buyer, being unfamiliar with these question, looks around and says, *"I am."* You then think there is no way anyone would put this person in charge of anything, let alone a decision like this. Of course you cannot say this, but you are certainly thinking it. You are also now stuck. This person has said he or she is in charge, and if you need to go around this person, you've got a problem because that person has told you he or she is in charge. If you want to go see a higher-level manager, a Russian for instance, you now have to figure out a stealthy way of doing it. Forget about *who;* ask *what*. The only question under Money is *what*, for a variety of reasons:

- ♦ ***What* is a process question, and companies work in processes.** *"What's the process for a budget?"* not, *"Do you have a budget?"* It really doesn't matter if they have a budget or not. Budgets are fluid at a senior management level. If the value on the investment they are making for your solution is high enough, they'll go get more budget money from someone or somewhere else. Vice presidents and C-level managers can always find more budget; lower-level managers can only spend what their superiors give them. You want to know the process of getting budget money, not what the budget is. If you work to their fixed budget, who is really in control?

- ♦ ***What* encourages discussion and gets more information.** *Who* questions limit the discussion to people. *What* questions focus the discussion on people, process, and who has the power. You can gather more information with what questions.

- ♦ ***What* describes a process and gives you a look at the entire picture.** *Who* is a point answer—you can answer it with one name.

- ♦ ***What* can include you; *who* cannot.** You may want to know if prospects are including you in their buy process.

♦ ***What* can be revisited at every call.** You can ask about changes to the process and even suggest changes. It is tough to suggest changes while asking *who.*

Money questions are overall process questions. You want to know, What is the overall process:

♦ To obtain funds?
♦ To make a decision within the organization?
♦ The committee is going to take in making a decision?

You get more bang for the buck with *what.*

Method

The first M, Money, has been addressed, and you now have some questions in your sales toolbox that will help you determine whether you have a qualified deal.

Method, the second M, focuses its questions on the buyer's specific process.

There are three questions that need to be answered in Method:

♦ What is the Implementation Date?
♦ What are the steps in the Buy/Sell process?
♦ What are the decision criteria?

Question #2: What Is the Implementation Date?

Nothing kills a sale like a maybe. Yeses are great; both you and the prospect win. Nos are great also; they let you know you are doing something wrong, and you can fix it. It's the maybes that will kill you. A maybe is the prospect's way of getting and maintaining control of the deal. The truth is that the Law of Sales Control discussed at the beginning of Chapter 1 states that if the prospect is in control, they are talking to someone else, and that other person is in control.

They don't get back to you in a timely manner. Meetings slip. It takes days for e-mails to be answered, if at all. You end up wondering if this sale is ever going to close. The answer is yes it will close—and it will close without you.

It's time to be ProActive. It's time to qualify this deal to see if you are in control or not. It's time to kill the maybes! The tool you are going to use to gain control back and destroy maybes is called the Implementation Date[Tool] (see Figure 9-2).

TOOL   **Implementation Date**[Tool]

Salespeople have been taught to focus on the wrong date. Assume you are currently in a sale. You began the sale a little while ago, and you see the end of the Buy/Sell process coming up soon—that end date when the prospect is going to make a decision. You know exactly what happens on that date. The prospect is going to sign the order, you get the order, you are happy, your boss is happy, and everybody wins. Except you have the wrong date.

The "Prospect expects to close" date is a seller's term, not a prospect's. Prospects could care less when they sign an order. Signing an order is just getting the P.O. out of purchasing, part of a process. What prospects really care about is the *Implementation Date*.

> *"What date do you plan to start using or implementing what we are talking about?"*

Figure 9-2 Implementation Date[Tool]

"When do you want to have the solution up and running?"

"What date does the financial justification start from?"

The Implementation Date, or I-Date, is when prospects want what they have ordered on their desk or when they are going to start using what you are trying to sell them. It could be defined as the date they start making money from the investment you are offering, when they can load it on their computer, have it on their dock, or start to implement the benefits that you are offering. The date the contract is signed is secondary compared with the date they have what you are selling them in their possession so they can start doing their job. This is what the prospect cares about; they care about their Implementation Date.

I-Dates: Do You Really Care?

Which date is significant to you?

♦ When you bought the shoes, or when you had them on your feet and could wear them to that special event?

♦ When you paid for the vacation, or when you went on it?

♦ When you bought the big-screen TV, or when you had it set up and started to watch it?

Prospects place importance on I-Dates more than any other date in the Buy/Sell process for the following reasons:

♦ It's when they promised their boss something would change.

♦ It's when they have scheduled other activities to commence (kick-off meetings, training, launch of something else that coincides with your product being implemented).

♦ Their customer is involved, or their customer's time line is involved.

♦ A schedule must be met.

♦ The company or department will increase their risk if they do not acquire what you are selling them.

♦ There's a deadline for another project for which your item is on the critical path.

♦   There's political pressure on something that your product/service is a part of.

There are a host of reasons that can tie what you are offering to an Implementation Date. Rest assured, your prospect has an I-Date. It's very important to know that an Implementation Date and that a Contract Close or Contract Sign date are different dates. They have to be, since they are coming from two perspectives, the seller's and the prospect's. Each party is approaching this deal differently and has a different reason for this deal to conclude. The salesperson wants to know when the sale ends; prospects want to know when they can start.

Can the I-Date and the Contract Signing Date be the same date? Of course they can, if the prospect needs what the salesperson is selling that day. Movie tickets, last-minute shopping, and impulse buying are examples of instant sale/use. For the most part, when you are selling a big-ticket item to a company or corporation, and there are many different departments and processes that need to approve the sale, these two dates will be different. From a ProActive sales perspective, assume that for 90+ percent of sales in progress the I-Date and the contract signing dates are different.

The Implementation Date is the "maybe killer." All qualified deals will have an I-Date. Salespeople usually know the I-Date in less than 50 percent of their current prospecting forecasts. There are three reasons for this.

1.   Salespeople are focused on the selling process and do not know about a Buy/Sell process.
2.   They don't think like a buyer and therefore focus on selling. They focus on the contract signing as the closing event for both parties.
3.   They don't ask for the I-Date, assuming instead that it is ASAP.

In the worst-case scenario, the salesperson tries to juxtapose the buyer's I-Date to match the seller's Contract Sign Date, which usually happens at the end of a year, the end of a quarter, or the end of a month (no surprise there).

"If you sign by the end of the month, we can give you an additional 10 percent off."

This is an example of an out-of-control sale for two reasons. First, the salesperson is focusing on the Contract Sign Date, not the Implementation Date. Second, because the salesperson cannot think like a buyer, he or she has to give a discount and buy the sale, a costly selling skill deficiency. What the ProActive salesperson would say in this case would be:

> "Ms. Meyers, you have stated you would like this up and running by the fifteenth. Is there anything that would prevent us executing this agreement today and therefore giving you a two-week cushion to make sure the implementation goes as smoothly as possible (risk)?"

This salesperson is thinking and selling in a Buy/Sell perspective. Using the I-Date tool will help you stay focused on the buyer's concerns, which must always take precedence if you are to win the sale. Let's see what else is important.

Question #3: What Are the Steps in the Buy/Sell Process?

This is the second vital question under Method. As we discussed above, knowing the buyer's I-Date can make or break a sales forecast. The I-Date is a very important tool, but it does have a limitation. The I-Date ensures a commitment by the prospect, where getting a commitment is a good thing to have. What the I-Date does *not* do is tell you how the prospect is going to buy. It does not give you the steps in the Buy/Sell process the buyer is going to go through or information on what direction the buyer is going to buy in—and buyers do buy in a direction. The BBB—Buyers Buy Backwards^{Tool}, discussed later in this chapter, gives you the buyer's buying direction.

Finding out the steps in the process is important so that the salesperson and the prospect can agree on how to get from where they are today to where they want to be tomorrow. The problem is that most salespeople want the buyer to adapt to the salesperson's process and, at the end, close. Prospects are different, and at the end they "make a decision"; they do not "close." Even worse, the reactive salesperson wants prospects to follow their sales cycle, which of course prospects don't want to do for two reasons: first, because it is not theirs, and second, it goes in the wrong direction—it goes forwards instead of backwards.

Salespeople sell forwards, but buyers buy backwards (see Figure 9-3).

Selling Forwards

Have you ever said something like this?

> "OK, we are at the Educate step in this sale right now. What I want to do next is to schedule a meeting to complete the Educate process, and we should be done with that by the end of next week. Then I'll give a demonstration so ownership transfers, which should complete the Validate step by the twenty-eighth. We can then complete the proposal by the following tenth, so they will make a decision by the end of next month. These are the steps I see the prospect taking for us to get to the close."

And how successful were you? Honestly now.

Unfortunately, many salespeople think this way. Selling forwards is inherent in almost all sales strategies.

Salespeople and their managers get together and discuss where a prospect is within a sales cycle and what the next steps are, so that the sales manager knows what to expect and where he or she can add value.

Figure 9-3 Method: Backwards or Forwards?

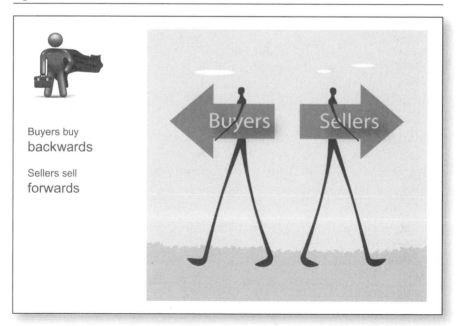

Buyers buy
backwards

Sellers sell
forwards

When does the salesperson think they are going to close this order, since it is on the sales forecast, and the sales manager wants to get this deal by the end of the quarter? Do the salesperson's steps make sense? Has the salesperson presented these steps to the prospect, and has the prospect agreed? Does the sales manager have anything to add to the steps the salesperson has proposed so the sales cycle can be shortened or the competitive situation for this deal lessened?

Does this sound like a typical conversation you would have with your boss? The problem is that it goes in the wrong direction. Salespeople sell forwards, but buyers buy backwards.

Salespeople are trained to think of a next step, then the next step, then the one after that, and so on, all the way until a close. This is good thinking. *Proactive Selling*'s Summarize, Bridge, and Pull^{Tool} is always pulling to a next step as well. However, next-step selling must be based on the prospect's *buy cycle*, not on the seller's sell cycle. Buyers buy backwards, not forwards.

Think about it. When was the last time you purchased anything of some importance? You bought it backwards.

- **Last car:** The lease on my car is running out on this date, so I need to do something about that soon.
- **Last vacation:** OK, we have to go on vacation the week of July 10. That is the only week all the kids are free. We need to finalize our plans soon.
- **Last party:** The surprise birthday party is going to be on the twentieth. We need to get the invitations out three weeks in advance, so we need to decide soon where it is going to be.

Last house, last set of golf clubs, last business suit, last computer, last . . . you get the point. Buyers start from a date, usually the Implementation Date, and they go backwards from there. Here's a typical conversation that goes on in a company, with individuals, the buyer, and anyone in the company who is involved in the decision, to make sure the Implementation Date can be met or needs adjustment.

"OK, folks, we have to have this computer system up and running by July 7. That's four months away. What has to happen between then and now to make this happen?"

The group has a discussion on what has to happen. Purchasing has to be involved. The system specifications have to be finalized. The system has to be chosen among three vendors. Training has to be scheduled. There has to be time for senior management approval. The list goes on and on. The next conversation goes like this.

> "Good, we now have a list of twenty things that have to happen between now and July 7. Let's map these out to make sure we can get all the things we need to do done, so we feel good about making our July 7 date."

Buyers start from a date and go backwards. Once they have all the tasks and activities they need, they go backwards and adjust the schedule accordingly if they need to.

> "I just can't make a decision this week because I won't have time to review the hardware implementation plan. I can get to it next week though, and it should not impact that July 7 date on this end."

This statement is a backwards statement. The buyer thought about what needed to get done, figured out how long she would need, and chose a date. Once the date was chosen, the buyer thought backwards to make sure there were no other conflicts, and that she had enough time to make the July 7 date (Implementation Date).

Dragons

The thing that really makes I-Dates effective is that they are important to the customer, which is why salespeople tend not to pay too much attention to them. Salespeople really care about "getting the order," and focus on the customer signing the order, releasing the purchase order, or cutting the check. ProActive salespeople care about I-Dates, and the events or commitments that go along with I-Dates to make sure they do not slip, the critical events or commitments we call dragons.

Say your customer has told you their I-Date is August 14. Of course you ask, *"Why the 14th?"*

If you heard, *"I don't know if we're firm on that date. We're really shooting for the end of summer,"* then you know you've met an I-Date without a strong dragon.

So what is a dragon? A dragon is an important event or significant pain point; it drives the Business Case Buyer's needs. Dragons are the real reasons the customer is willing to change. They are the "mission-critical factors" and probably the only reason the upper-management customer is talking to you (see Figure 9-4).

Dragons are Russian in nature. They include mandates like:

> *"We've got to increase new product speed-to-market by 20 percent. Our competition is going to leapfrog us and we need to do this so we don't lose market share."*

> *"The new CFO insists every plant reduce costs by 15 percent. We have three months to submit this new budget. How are we going to do this?"*

> *"The new CEO has promised Wall Street this week that he will increase sales by 20 percent. Time to look at Plan B."*

So, what have we learned from the mediocre response to our question above about the I-Date? That dragon sure isn't breathing much fire. This tells us that the I-Date is not too firm, and therefore your forecast date is probably going to slip. If, however, you heard the customer say,

> "The 14th is a firm day. We have five employees flying in from all our other plants for our product launch, and we need your product to be up and running for that meeting. Additionally, my boss, Mary, has committed to the CEO that she will be in town on the 14th to kick off the meeting and personally discuss the reason we're switching to your product."

OK, you now see that the 14th is an absolutely critical day. There are a lot of things, events, commitments—dragons—that are tied to the I-Date of August 14. The possibility of the 14th slipping is remote, since airfares, schedules, and commitments would have to be redone and rescheduled . . . a big pain, so not likely to happen.

The I-Date is secure, and if you back up from that I-Date, so is the Contract Signing Date—so your forecast of that deal coming in on July 30 is looking good.

A few dragon rules:

♦ Every solid I-Date has at least two dragons. Most salespeople usually stop at one and are happy. However, get two and that date won't slip.

♦ No dragons, no I-Date. No I-Date, no real deal.

♦ A fire-breathing dragon is a commitment by the most senior person involved in the sale to *their* boss regarding an event that includes what you are selling.

♦ An I-Date is not about them buying your product or service. It's about how and when they are going to use it, and the events and commitments that are anchored to it.

So put on that helmet, get on that horse, and go find those dragons. An I Date without dragons is like the sun rising in the west . . . it just doesn't happen.

Now you have a problem. Salespeople make a sales call with their selling steps planned forward and present this process to the buyer. The prospect typically can understand what a salesperson is talking about, since all salespeople talk forwards, and prospects are used to translating the forward discussion and then seeing if it fits into the backward process they have committed to. When prospects have to translate what you are saying into what they need to know, you have lost control of the sale.

To compound the problem, in the sales presentation the salesperson is proposing a next step. The buyer typically agrees with the salesperson's next step, the salesperson feels confident, asks for the next step, and the buyer agrees. The salesperson leaves feeling very good believing he or she is in control. They are in control, but of the wrong process.

Figure 9-4 I-Date with Dragons

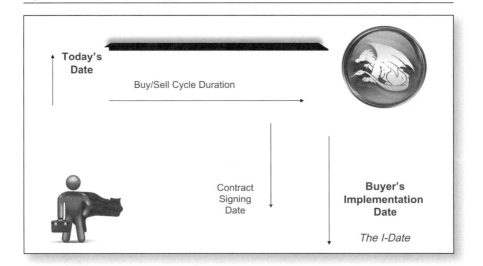

They are in control of the selling process, which of course the prospect has no commitment to, nor does the buyer have any ownership of it. They have their own process.

Now, after the salesperson leaves, the buyer typically takes what the salesperson has proposed and tries to fit it into the buy process. If it comes close to matching, the buyer will feel good. If it does not, a salesperson may be eliminated from the process because the selling and buying processes did not match up, regardless of features and benefits. Worse yet, the prospect is always neutral, so who is in control now? It's not you, but your competition.

TOOL **BBB—Buyers Buy Backwards**^Tool

A ProActive salesperson must control the process and understand there is a buying process out there. BBB is a tool that states the salesperson must:

1. Understand that the buyer's process starts from the Implementation Date.
2. Identify the tasks and activities that the prospect has to accomplish.
3. Take the buyer's process and go backwards from the I-Date. Then, once completed, overlay the sales process with the buy process, and present this to the prospect for mutual agreement.

The prospect may then agree, may need to change some things, get some approvals, or do whatever he or she needs to do to formalize the process. If this sounds a lot like the SalesMap^Tool, from Chapter 7, that's because it is. And *you* are now the one in control. You have taken the time to understand the prospect's buy process and even helped the prospect to identify some things that were missed, based on the selling organization's experience with other customers.

Once the buy process is mapped out, the salesperson identifies the selling process, the things the selling organization needs to do, and the timeframe in which these tasks can be accomplished. (Too many sales are lost with, *"Quick, we need a full demo of the system by next Monday. Who can we get, and how fast can we free up the schedule?"*) Armed with the buy process and the selling process, the ProActive salesperson can now overlay the two, look for discrepancies, fix these, and agree with the prospect on what needs to get done and by when.

The prospect feels good because the Implementation Date was used, not a selling or contract signing date. The prospect also feels good because the process has been identified from both sides. He or she believes all the bases have been covered, and their risk level has now decreased with this vendor, regardless of features and benefits. The salesperson is in control.

Buyers buy backwards, and salespeople sell forwards. It is the ProActive salesperson's job to:

- Identify the prospects' Implementation Date.
- Identify the tasks and activities the prospect has to accomplish.
- Identify what the selling organization needs to do.
- Get agreement from the prospect on all the activities.
- Eliminate any translation the prospect used to do when he or she was presented a sales cycle.
- Make the translation of the buying and selling processes a mutual process, with the salesperson playing the conductor.

Control the process, win the deal. Since the ProActive sell process is based on the prospect's Implementation Date, the odds this deal will close, and close when the sales forecast says it will come in, are well above 50 percent, probably closer to 80 to 90 percent. Remember: BBB—Buyers Buy Backwards.

The GETS Chart: Buyers Buy Backwards Example

Very early in my selling career, the B.F. Goodrich Company was looking for some custom software development work to help its phone system track and allocate costs to incoming and outgoing phone calls for departmental budgeting reasons. There were three vendors bidding on this business, and we were one.

Vendors had to give a presentation on who they were and what they could do for Goodrich. We flew in two senior consultants to help make a presentation to Goodrich, and our meeting lasted more than two hours. We went back to the office and discussed what had happened.

During the meeting, Goodrich had discussed with us what they had to do on their part to make their I-Date, and we told them what we would have to do to make that date. Goodrich had laid out over thirty tasks that needed to be accomplished, and we had close to the same number. Sixty activities were laid out, and then it was time for the consultants to catch their flight back home.

The next day, I was looking at all these activities, and I had no idea what to do. I am a salesperson, not a project manager. Well, there happened to be a project management consultant in my office named Otto Bufe. Otto had walked by my cube and inquired on what I was doing, and I explained. Otto then remarked, "Oh, that's a PERT (Program Evaluation and Review Technique) chart."

Otto proceeded to take the 60+ "data points" and input them into a charting program. We assigned time lengths to each activity and ordered them according to which had to be accomplished first, second, and so on. We worked backwards from the prospect's I-Date and Otto then ran the PERT program, and out came this color chart, complete with a critical path, which we plotted on large chart paper. Goodrich's activities were on the top of the chart, ours were on the bottom, and the timeline was in the middle.

The following Monday, I took the chart down to Goodrich, and we had a lively conversation around the chart itself. We adjusted activities, moved dates around, and reworked the chart. I went back to the office, Otto ran the program with the revised activities/dates, and I sent the new chart to our consultants. They reworked their activities, Otto ran another chart, and a few days later, I went to Goodrich to get their buy-in.

They were extremely pleased. They could see what they needed to do, and by when. It made their life simpler and lowered their risk of the unknown. They adjusted a few things, I went back to the office, and Otto ran yet another chart.

The evaluation and vendor selection took about five weeks. Twice a week, I would go down to Goodrich and discuss the chart. Internally at Goodrich, the project was known as GETS (Goodrich Electronic Tracking System). The chart became known as the GETS Chart.

I had no idea what my competitors were doing, or how much they were bidding for this project. I only knew I had the GETS Chart. Goodrich used the GETS Chart in its internal meetings with their management to get final approval of the project. Since our activities were shown on the GETS Chart as well, it became a nontransferable competitive advantage. Other vendors would have great difficulty plugging their activities into our methodology. Goodrich wanted GETS. We had the Goodrich's Implementation Date, we had their process backwards, we had our process forwards, we had mutual buy-in, and we had the GETS Chart. We controlled the process and won the order.

There are countless numbers of GETS Chart examples. ProActive selling means that if you own the process, you own the deal. The GETS example is just one way of gaining and keeping control of the process.

We have looked at the first two of the three Method questions that the ProActive salesperson must get answers to: What is the I-Date, and what are the steps in the prospect's Buy/Sell process? Now let's take a look at the third: What are the decision criteria?

Question #4: What Are the Decision Criteria?

What are the reasons buyers buy? There are hundreds of reasons prospects will end up buying from you, but in many cases, they end up buying for different reasons (see Figure 9-5). It seems that many features/benefits are evaluated during the Buy/Sell process, and in the end the prospect buys for only two or three of these reasons. The PPPII^{Tool} allows you to focus on the right two or three reasons and concentrate your efforts.

TOOL | **PPPII**^{Tool}

A prospect's buying decision comes down to five criteria. A decision to buy a good or service ends up focusing on:

1. *P*roduct/service features and benefits
2. *P*roduct quality
3. *P*rofessional support (also called "ease of use")
4. *I*nvestment
5. *I*mage

This is your buying pie, your PPPII, the five criteria on which a prospect will make a decision. In these five areas lie 99 percent or more of the buying reasons your prospect will use to make a decision to select you as a vendor or not.

1. Product Features and Benefits: This is the easy one. Salespeople can list pages and pages of items on these. Many of them have a competitive slant, rather than a prospect slant. Please remember the Law of Competitive Selling.

Figure 9-5 Method: Decision Criteria

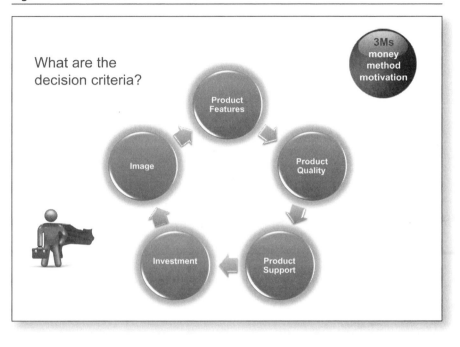

THE LAW OF COMPETITIVE SELLING

Buyers buy for their own reasons, not how you stack up on a competitive issue. They don't care about your competitive issues. Demonstrate the Feature/Benefit/Value you provide and how it matches up against prospects' requirements and their competitive issues, not how you do things better/cheaper/faster than a competitor.

Features/benefits and the value they provide are what are important in most sales presentations. Remember to stress the benefits, not just list hundreds of features and hope the prospect can sort them out and pick a few good ones. It's the reactive salesperson who wants to Spray and Pray, hoping that if she gets enough features of what they do out in front of the prospect, that prospect will be able to pick out the ones that are important to him. The reactive salesperson's motto is:

"Better to discuss too many features and overwhelm the prospect than to risk leaving something out."

This is reactive hit-and-miss selling. The ProActive salesperson does his or her homework, determines the needs of the prospect in discussions with the prospect, and then discusses features/benefits and value. ProActive salespeople also de-emphasize features that are not important to the prospect, regardless of how important these features are to the salesperson. Too many car salespeople show customers the car engine, even when those buyers tell the salesperson they don't give a fig about the engine. For some fun, next time you are shopping for a car and see a reactive car salesperson who just has to show you the engine, let him. When the salesperson opens the hood of the car, exclaim, *"Yep, that's an engine alright. I wondered what was under that hood. By the way, it's a pretty engine too."* This is a perfect response to a reactive salesperson.

The benefits are what count, but the features anchor the prospect, so make sure you state the feature and the benefit, as well as the value. You will find that, in most sales, it gets down to fewer than three features that are important. Work with the prospect to determine what they are, rather than be a reactive list generator.

2. **Product Quality:** Prospects look for quality when buying. How well is the product made, how will it stand up, how does it compare to similar products, and is the quality difference (towards or away) worth the price difference? These are some of the questions prospects ask themselves. The prospect's interest in quality breaks down into five areas:

♦   **Good Enough Quality:** This is quality adequate to meet the need. If a prospect is looking for a product that merely meets the need, quality is usually medium to low in terms of importance. Emotion has not yet entered into the evaluation, but in all likelihood, it will. If a prospect is interested only in "good enough quality," you can educate that prospect and move this priority higher within a prospective sale.

♦   **The Best Quality:** If the prospect suggests that she needs "the best quality," quality is obviously high on her list of reasons to buy. Emotional as well as logical business reasons are in play, and the prospect has chosen to allow emotions to dominate the value equation.

♦   **Comparative Quality:** If the prospect is looking for only comparative quality, quality has not entered the decision process as an important factor, and probably will never be high up the priority list for a number of reasons. Usually, it's because one of the other PPPII factors is so dominant. It's very hard to move someone in this area, since his or her other decision criteria are so high. You could spend a lot of time in this area, win the quality battle, and lose the war.

♦ **Time Quality:** Time quality prospects play the short term vs. long term debate to the maximum. *"How long will I have it?"*

"How long will I keep it?"

"How long will it be in use?"

"When will I not need it anymore?"

"When will I be replacing it?"

These are questions prospects ask when they view quality over time. Prospects who have a time definition to quality have to measure quality over time, and the astute salesperson addresses these quality/time issues.

♦ **Yesterday Quality:** Here prospects assume quality based on history, image, reputation, personal use, or a host of other reasons. This assumed quality usually addresses the issue of risk. It is based on emotional logic and has no firm roots. A yesterday quality objection is one that is easily addressed if you take the high ground. You can introduce new information or discuss what has changed in the past year or so to overcome poor quality or reinforce good quality.

3. Product Support/Ease of Use: Product support/ease of use implies the service and support the prospect will be getting from the selling organization. This can take many forms:

Training	24/7 support	Extended warranty
Installation	Hand holding	User interface
Warranty	Certification process	Instruction manuals
Repair	Customer support	and documentation
Engagement	Educational	
models	experience	

And more. Buyers want to feel they:

1. Will be taken care of (support for the risk element).
2. Can maximize their value (ease of use for the investment element).

If prospects emphasize professional support/ease of use, it's because they are going to put the product/service to maximum use, or because they are going into uncharted waters. In either case, if they need assistance while using it, there must be someone available to them to help them out. These two issues speak volumes to Investment and Risk, two big points on the ValueStar. Buyers want to get the most they can, but there is a balance between support (risk) and investment.

> ## The Value Axiom
> You can tell me what you want, and I will tell you how much it is, or you can tell me how much you want to spend, and I will tell you what you can buy. However, you cannot tell me what you want and how much you want to spend.

If you want a 25 percent discount at a retail clothing store, you cannot expect the same kind of service you would get at a high-quality retail store where you pay full price. The manual and instructions for the $7,000 plasma screen TV will be very different than for the $99.00 9-inch portable TV. The instructions and support you get with the $29.99 software package are different from those of the $499.95 package. Buyers expect service and support when they pay a premium price. They expect a top-notch service organization. Satisfaction is directly related to their expectations, and because expectations of different prospects differ so widely, this is the area in which you can really make a competitive difference.

Buyers assume a lot, and they assume a similar level of professional support/ease of use from all vendors. All car dealers' services are the same. All retail, software, hardware, airlines, clothing, consulting, insurance, hotels, sporting goods, and electronic companies have the same service, right? Wrong! KPMG is not the same as Ernst and Young. Dell and Hewlett-Packard are very dissimilar. Service, ease of use, and ease of doing business instill a unique kind of brand loyalty. It is the ProActive salesperson who knows that professional support/ease of use is a great differentiator in the prospect's mind at all levels within the prospect's organization. Since you are the one who brings up the benefit and how what you offer supplies the benefit they are going to receive, it becomes a nontransferable competitive exclusive.

> *"You are asking for 24/7 help desk support. We offer that, in this manner . . ."*
>
> *"You want a company that can provide you up-to-the-minute information, and here's how we would do this for you."*
>
> *"Hello, this is the ABC Company, and you are talking to a live person. May I help you?"*

These are three examples of how you can use professional support/ ease of use as an advantage. Emphasize the Features/Benefits/Value you offer that fall into this category, for they are competitive weapons in your sales process.

4. Investment: Investment is an area where you need to devote some quality time to preparation. With PPPII, Product Features is usually the category for which salespeople can generate a list that seems to go on and on. Product Quality and Professional Support are the ones that usually get the most discussion because they relate to the prospect's interest in your goods and services. Investment, however, seems to be the one for which most salespeople have the shortest bulleted list, because it requires you to think like a buyer.

Prospects are not buying your product because it is neat, cool, the latest rage, or something they can't live without. In this competitive market, there are so many alternatives to choose from that it can get confusing to a buyer to decide on the best investment of their resources. Buyers end up asking themselves two sets of questions. First, they ask themselves the *extremes* questions:

> *"What do we need to pay more or less attention to?"*
>
> *"What do I need to increase or decrease?"*
>
> *"What do I need to amplify or diminish?"*
>
> *"What do I need extra of or a reduced amount of?"*
>
> *"Do I need it now or later?"*

Salespeople must always be able to answer extremes questions. By having your solution, product, or service, what will the prospect get more of or less of? All a prospect wants to do is increase something or decrease something.

The second set of questions buyers then ask themselves are the *how much* questions. In other words, extremes questions must be quantifiable. If you don't get into specifics on what you are offering when addressing the extremes questions, your product or service will be viewed as a commodity. *"It will increase your productivity"* is a commodity statement, because it provides no quantitative value. To address the Investment issue, your statements must be quantifiable. *"It will increase your productivity by 25 percent over 2 years"* is an Investment statement. Typical Investment comments are:

> *"Decrease time to market by 3 months."*
> *"Decrease your overhead by 17 percent annually."*
> *"Increase your market share by 2 points within 12 months."*
> *"Improve your margin on this product by 3 percent this fiscal year."*
> *"Increase production by 30,000 units/month."*

These are quantifiable monetary statements that Investment statements should speak to. Your product or service must address the Investment issue, and it must do so in a quantifiable way for it to be of any value to a vice president, let alone a CEO.

Answer these two questions for every sale:

1. What extremes is the prospect trying to solve?
2. By how much?

It's about now that many salespeople say,

"Our product, however, doesn't make that big of an impact for our customers. How can we make such a big difference?"

The answer is obvious. Your prospect is willing to invest resources and spend money with you. So *it must be the case* that you make a difference to them.

Prospects are greedy; they want their money back, which is why they would give you any money in the first place. Your product does make a difference. It may not be the thing that gives the company a great return on a total investment it is making, but it is a very important piece of the whole. Find out the return the prospect is expecting from the whole (do you remember the Solution Box^Tool in Chapter 8? You always want to work your way into Solution Box B), and then go from there. Do not be whittled down either. If a prospect is going to be saving $1,000,000/year with a specific project that your product is just a small piece of, your return is not only the value you add but also the value of the entire project.

Your specific product/service may be worth a $10,000/year savings to the company, but with you in the equation, the larger $1,000,000/year has a greater degree of certainty to it. If someone else is in the picture other than you, the unknown factor increases, which means greater risk, and you know how buyers hate risk. The $1,000,000/year project has just become riskier, which upper-level management hates.

Risk costs money. Do not let the prospect control the sales cycle and start dictating to you what you are worth. PPPII, especially Investment, is meant to move you from being a seller to becoming a financial partner with the buyer. Find out, quantitatively, what you are worth. Prospects know the numbers; all you have to do is ask the right questions.

5. Image: The final *I* in PPPII stands for Image. Image or Brand is still very important. It is why people still spend more money on shirts that have a horse and polo player on them than they do for a shirt that doesn't have that logo. Image is the emotional play, and this is a very WIIFM area, so it therefore should be probed as such. Image can be obtained from many different areas:

- Company: Length in business, size, geographic location
- Product: Features, benefits, most used, competitive advantage
- Customers: Certain industries, certain market verticals, showcase accounts
- Processes: ISO 9002, industry certifications, educational certifications
- Logo: Brand recognition, partnership recognition, trademarks and patents
- History: Length Years in business, number of firsts, number of bests, reputation, stability

Image has many different categories. What is important to understand is WIIFM. You must be the one who helps prospects with their image. Look at the preceding Image list and switch your focus to the prospects. How can you help them with their image? They want to improve their image, from one perspective or another, be it the company, product, process, partnership, or something else. It's your job to make sure they see the value of doing business with you from *their* side, not yours. The fact you have been in business for twenty-three years is good, but from the prospect's image perspective, they could care less. They want to be seen as doing business with only reputable firms, not any "the latest fad" suppliers. The fact that you've been in business that long may mean a lot to you, but its importance to them is that it helps them with *their* image. Image is not just what you think of yourself, or what the prospect thinks of you. It's about what the prospect thinks of themselves, and quite frankly, they are certainly more interested in themselves than they are in you. Image needs to be looked at from both sides, not just what you have to offer.

Here are five rules to follow when you are using PPPII:

1. Take the "So What" Quiz. All PPPII questions must answer the "So What" quiz; it quantifies the PPPII questions.

> "Mr. Smith will be more productive because of the quality of our product and support."
> "So what?"
> "He will be able to cut costs."
> "So what?"
> "He said that cutting costs is his number one priority."
> "So what?"
> "He'll be able to report to his boss that he's cutting 22 percent of his overhead budget over the next two years, which is above his stated goal."

"So what" questions are meant to quantify. In the above example, too many sales managers would allow the salesperson to stop at the first statement: since both the sales manager and the salesperson are very proud of their quality and support, it must be obvious to the prospect as well. This is thinking like a seller, and not like a buyer. "So what" questions make sure you really are thinking like a buyer. PPPII sets the stage. It puts you in the right ball field. "So what" questions make sure you remember that it is a Buy/Sell cycle, not the other way around. You want to probe as deep as you can into the answers given to you until you get the real answers from the prospect. Asking, "So what would that mean to you?" questions will help clarify the answers the prospect is giving you.

2. Ask great questions. PPPII can be a great tool. Most salespeople end up having 20 to 30 things under each of these five categories. They don't want to leave anything to chance, and they want to be prepared. Great salespeople ask great questions, and PPPII is a great way for a ProActive salesperson to focus the sales call, and ask the right questions.

Which of the following questions will elicit more information?

1. *"Well Ms. Hamilton, what are you looking for?"*
2. *"Well Ms. Hamilton, when it comes to the quality you require* (or *the amount of support that you will be needing), what is important to you?*

When you focus your questions on PPPII, you end up asking more pointed questions in an area to which the prospect wants to go, since PPPII is the prospect's decision criteria.

3. Focus on only one or two questions. Typically, a buyer focuses on one or two key criteria out of the five. Usually, the reasons have little to do with the product/service features. Sellers may sell with product features, but buyers buy for the other four reasons.

4. Think like a buyer. Having a list of PPPII things that you do and then having that same list in terms of *what they mean for the prospect* will give you a tremendous competitive advantage. Period. Your competition will not have an extensive list like PPPII. You will win because you have covered all areas and can easily access the few that are important to the prospect. Fill out PPPII from the buyer's perspective for a competitive advantage.

5. Be fluent in all three languages. You should have a PPPII in Spanish, Russian, and Greek. You never know who you are going to end up talking to; you never know when you'll need to address a User Buyer and when a Business Case Buyer.

The last question under Method—What are the decision criteria?—is a very important question. It focuses you on the buyer's perspective rather than the seller's. It makes you ask great questions rather than blurt out answers, which ProActive salespeople would never do. It makes buyers quantify the investment they are making to you. It prepares you for sales calls because it will make you focus on what is really important to the prospect other than just features.

Motivation

The final three of our seven qualifying questions come under the topic of Motivation. What is really motivating the prospects to do something, and can you satisfy their need? The questions are:

♦ Is there a need?

♦ Can you meet that need?

♦ What does the prospect believe are the top two benefits with your solution?

These three questions will finalize the MMM qualification process.

Question #5: Is There a Need?

Is there a real need for your product or service, not an imaginary one, or one for which the salesperson can see the need but the prospect cannot? What has the prospect said her need is? A real need must address these issues:

♦ What is the reason for this need? (This is usually expressed in a TOWARDS or AWAY direction.)

♦ How much attention is this getting? (This goes back to knowing the process.)

♦ What is the final outcome? (What is going to change once a solution is put into place?)

♦ How much is it worth? (What is the financial or emotional gain?)

When these questions are answered, you have a legitimate need.

Question #6: Can You Meet that Need?

Can you really meet this need? To elaborate, you must have the knowledge of how, when, why, and what (actually, two whats).

♦ How can you meet the need—and does the prospect agree with you?

♦ When does the prospect say he will implement a solution—and does this agree with the Implementation Date?

♦ Why would the prospect implement a solution?

- ♦ What is the overriding business case?
- ♦ What increases or decreases, and by how much?

Meeting the need is not just product fit. You must meet the business case need, the product fit need, and the process fit need. The sales world is full of unsigned sales deals because one or two of the above needs were unanswered. Can you meet *all* the customer's needs is the right question here. Remember, these are the *customer's* questions:

Business Case: What is the ROI? What is the Risk? What Return on Assets are we getting?

Product Fit: Does the product do what we want it to do? Is it the best of breed? Can it be leveraged into other areas?

Process Fit: How does this fit with the way we are currently doing business? How much do we have to change the way we do things because of this? Can we make things more efficient? What other departments will this affect? Will communication change because of this change we are making?

All of the need questions have to be addressed for you to have a qualified prospect and a fit of your product/service to the prospect's needs.

And now we move to the final qualifying question you will want to answer as you move forward in the qualifying process.

Question #7: What Does the Prospect Believe Are the Top Two Benefits with Your Solution?

What are the top two reasons for which the prospect has actually said he or she would purchase your product/service? It should be not just any solution, or the overall solution, but your specific solution. What has the prospect said, specifically, in their own words, about why they would make an investment with you? It must come from the prospect. Too many sales have been lost with,

"I haven't asked specifically, but I'm sure they would say . . ."

Sorry, that doesn't count. What has the prospect actually *said* regarding why he or she would make a decision in your favor? At this point, salespeople usually ask the following questions:

"How do I know what they tell me is the real reason?"
"How do I know if they are telling me the truth?"

"How do I know what they tell me is what they really mean?"

"Can they tell me one thing and really mean another?"

"How will I know when they really mean what they say?"

The following tool will help answer these questions.

| TOOL | Three Levels of Why™ |

The Three Levels of Why™ provides a questioning technique that all good salespeople have mastered. It's a way for the salesperson to understand where the buyer is coming from (see Figure 9-6).

There is a *real* reason why you make a decision, why you choose one thing over another. There's a *real* reason for the watch you wear, the car you drive, the shoes you own.

People don't like to talk about their real reasons, so they rationalize their decisions. And people don't like to discuss their rationalizations openly, so they develop "rapport reasons" to tell others why they made the choices they made. A "rapport reason" is a simple answer that the person who asked the question can, at least at a superficial level, relate to—hence the word "rapport." And by the same token, a "rapport question" isn't necessarily one to which you want a real answer; it's part of socializing, of creating rapport: *"How are you?"*—*"Fine thanks, and you?"* Do these two people really care about each other's health, or are they just establishing rapport?

Rapport reasons are the simple answers people have ready to answer rapport questions.

"How are you feeling?"—*"Fine."*

"Why did you buy that camera?"—*"I needed one."*

"Where are you going on vacation this year?"—*"Somewhere warm."*

Rapport answers always sound good, but are at the top of the three levels of why, so there always is more to someone's decision process.

You can change behavior only down at the third level of why—the *real* reason, the *real* explanation of why. Rapport answers are typically what salespeople get when they ask questions in a sales environment. Good salespeople get down to the second level of why, and deal with rationalizations. ProActive salespeople know to go deeper and get to the third level of why. An example of Three Levels of Why:

Figure 9-6 Three Levels of Why^{Tool}

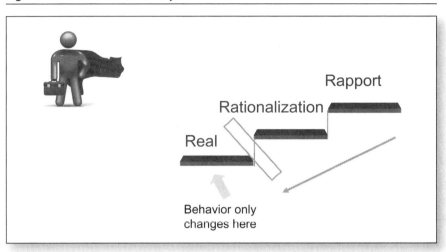

"That's a really nice watch you are wearing. Why did you buy that watch?" (First "why")

"I liked the color. I like a watch that has gold and silver." (Rapport response)

"I'm sure there were a lot of gold and silver watches. Why did you buy that watch?" (Second "why")

"I like the look. It is sporty, yet classic. I wanted a watch that you could wear every day, yet that would look good on special occasions." (Rationalization response)

"I am sure there were many watches that were sporty yet classic. Why did you buy that particular watch?" (Third "why")

"You want to know why, I'll tell you exactly why. I just got a promotion at work, and I have always wanted this brand of watch. I bought the watch because I earned it." (Real reason)

This is an example of Three Levels of Why, and shows the questioner getting to the real reason. If someone comes to your store looking for a new cooking set, you can see how helpful it would be to know the *real* reason they are in the market. That way, if you don't have the cooking set they are looking for, knowing the real reason allows you to better influence the buyer's behavior.

"I'm sorry I don't have the cooking set you're describing. I can tell that it's a good one. People who are really into cooking usually buy one of these two sets. Let me show you."

You now have a chance with this buyer because you know his or her real reasons for buying.

Three Levels of Why: The Beginning

I came up with the Three Levels of Why when I lost a deal. They say you learn more from your losses than your victories, and that's probably true.

I was selling computer-aided design and computer-aided manufacturing (CAD/CAM) systems many years ago. I was calling on a shop that made plastic injection molds for the auto industry, and they were one of the largest in the area. It had been an eight-month sales cycle, and the deal was worth about $500,000. We were up against our number one competitor, who had the largest market share, was dominant in my territory, and had ten times the sales volume we had.

I thought we had this deal done. We had done a good job, and I felt very secure in the probability we had for this sale. Our benchmark part, which both parties were required to do, looked so much better than theirs. I had posters and pictures of our CAD/CAM system in most of the engineers' cubes. This deal was ours for the taking.

Finally, the prospect company informed us they wanted to make a decision by the end of the week. They wanted one vendor to present Friday at 10:00 A.M., one to present at 1:00 P.M., and they would make a decision by 4:00 that very afternoon. I positioned us to go at 1:00 P.M., and made sure we had a copy of the agenda of what we were going to cover (and even had had that approved by them).

Thursday afternoon, I called the chief engineer to make sure there were no questions. I drove down to Akron to be at their facility to make sure there were no competitors lurking about. At 5:30, the chief engineer told me he was going home. I walked him to his car to make sure everything was going in our favor.

In the parking lot on the way to his car, he turned to me and asked me a question. *"Skip, do you and your system do XYZ as well as all the other things you have shown us?"*

This was a great question. He was asking about a feature that we had, but it had no relevance to him, since he was a mold shop and would never need feature XYZ. It was a competitor's strength, but I knew I could convince him he would be wasting his money on such a feature.

"Dave, yes we have that feature, but quite frankly, you'd never use it, and here's why . . .," I started in on my best sales pitch. *"You need to do business with a company that focuses its efforts on features that have relevance to you and*

what you need to do. Our company focuses on mold shops and has a great deal of understanding of the needs of companies like yours . . . blah, blah, blah." Dave agreed he would never need that XYZ feature. I had handled that objection perfectly.

The next day, our competitor gave his presentation at 10:00, we gave ours at 1:00, and at 4:00 we got a call saying they made a decision in favor of the competition.

I couldn't believe it. I was crushed. I knew I had the backing from everyone, so what happened? After a very rough weekend, Monday I called Dave and asked for a meeting. We ended up going to lunch, and over that meal, this conversation took place.

"Dave, what happened?"

"Well when it came down to it, we liked your competitor's price. We saw all things as equal, and we decided that since your competitor lowered his price so that it was 10 percent lower than yours, we went with him." I thought about that for a while, but it didn't fit. It didn't sound right.

"Dave, that doesn't sound right. Price never really entered into our conversations."

A few moments later, the conversation continued.

"Well, we really liked that one data entry feature they offered. We like the way an engineer enters data into their system better than yours."

I knew that was not completely true. The engineers who had participated in the demonstrations absolutely *loved* our data input method. This had to be a second-level rationalization. It just didn't make sense, so I pressed on.

"Dave, I'm sure that had something to do with it, but I need to know. What was the real *reason you chose the competition?"*

After a long pause, Dave continued.

"You want to know why we went with your competitor, I'll tell you exactly why. I wanted your system more than the one we purchased. So did my engineers. Our chairman was a bit nervous spending $500,000 on a CAD/CAM system, though. That is a big expenditure for a company like ours. Your competitor realized that and offered all their other software, outside of what we were buying, to us for free. That made our decision swing toward them."

"But Dave, that doesn't make sense. You are a mold shop. You'll never use all that other software, especially that XYZ feature. It doesn't relate at all to what you do."

"That's true, but our chairman figured out that we are going to be using the system only one shift per day. He has a lot of friends in the area who want to use a CAD/CAM system, but cannot afford it. So what we did was buy the system, load it with software that his friends can use, and then we are going to sell them

time on the computer system. This way, he defrays his initial cost for the system and lowers his overall risk of the investment. We bought from them because they offered all their other software for free."

At that point, I said something like, *"Well Dave, we can offer you that too!"* But it was too late.

In the parking lot the week before, when Dave asked me a question, I had done one of the stupidest things a salesperson can do. I answered his question without looking deeper. What I should have done is used Three Levels of Why to find the *real* reason why he was asking me that question. I might have saved the sale.

Best Use of Three Levels of Why

Three Levels of Why is a tool to be used when you are asking prospects questions about why they are making a decision, especially why they would buy from you. Ask them what are the top two reasons they would make a decision in your favor, and then use Three Levels of Why for each of those reasons. How will you know when you get to the third level of why? You'll know . . . the emotion, the passion comes out. You keep gently questioning until that passion and emotion comes to the surface.

"Why would you do that?"

"What would that mean to you?"

"So I think I hear you say this, is that correct?"

Emotion is at the third level of why, and you can argue that most if not all decisions are emotional first, then they are rationalized, and then rapport answers are created. Listen for their intensity, not just their words. A ProActive salesperson masters the Three Levels of Why to get to the real reason—the emotional reasons of why a prospect would make a decision.

MMM: The Seven Questions Reviewed

The questions that have been discussed in this chapter are the master qualification tools in the ProActive salesperson's toolbox. A qualified sales process is worth its weight in gold. There are many other qualification questions you can ask other than the seven listed here. It seems sometimes that you can never qualify a deal too much. The MMM qualification method is a way for a salesperson to get as much qualification information as he or she can in the beginning steps of the sale to make a logical business decision: "Should I continue on with this Buy/Sell process right now?" By knowing the answers to the MMM questions, and making sure those answers are positive toward your solution, the ProActive salesperson will have a better than 50 percent chance of winning the sale. Control the process, and you will control the sale. Control the process, qualify the prospect, and you will win more sales than ever before.

Here's the three-by-five version of the qualification process:

Money

1. What is the process:
   - To obtain budget (funds)?
   - To obtain a decision?

Method

2. What is the Implementation Date?
3. What are the steps in the Buy/Sell process?
4. What are the decision criteria?

Motivation

5. Is there a need?
6. Can I meet that need?
7. What does the prospect believe are the top two benefits with your solution?

CHAPTER 10

Validate

YOU'RE MAKING PROGRESS on controlling the process. You started the process with generating initial interest. You did your homework. You figured out when to call, who to call on, and where to spend your time. You've learned the three languages appropriate to three company levels, and you can now speak the right language to the right person all the time. Then, armed with your prepared 30-Second Speech, you made the first sales call. You got the prospect's attention and interest, then you Summarized, Bridged, and Pulled (SBPed) to the Education phase. You did a good job of sales education and, together with the prospect, developed a SalesMap. During the Initial Interest and Education stages, you were qualifying to MMM and the seven questions, and you now feel you have a better than 50 percent chance of winning this deal. You SBP from Educate, and now you are in the Validate stage.

The buyer now understands what you are offering, and you understand what the prospect needs. Each of you wants to take a next step. The problem is the steps may be different for each of you, and if you aren't careful, you can lose control of this sale, and potentially lose this deal.

You want to start closing this sale. You want to "put some numbers together" or "sit down and work something out" or "get together and see what makes sense." You figure:

"I now know what they need; they know what we offer. Everything looks good, so let's get this done."

Whoa, not so fast. Now is exactly the time to slow down. The prospect is not at that stage yet. He or she needs to understand what this solution is going to do for him or her, exactly how it is going to work, and exactly what the final benefits are going to be, both to the company and to the prospect personally (WIIFM). The prospect needs transfer of ownership; the seller needs to close this deal: This is a major accident waiting to happen.

The ProActive Initiation of Transfer of Ownership

At this point in the Buy/Sell process the prospect wants to understand what the solution is going to look like.

"What is this going to specifically do, and how will the results of what I am buying come to pass?"

"What will my world be like if the solution you are offering me actually comes into being?"

"What will be different?"

"What will change?"

"Will it really work as claimed?"

These are the kinds of questions prospects have at this time. It's the next step in their process. They don't want what the salesperson is offering right now: a proposal or a contract. They really don't. They might in fact agree to one now, but only because:

♦ You as a reactive salesperson are forcing one on them.

♦ They don't fully understand what you are selling, so they are hoping your proposal will shed more light on your product/service. (You are now in limbo. The prospect is still looking for more Education, and you're trying to Validate.)

- ◆ They need to know their options so they can envision the full solution. (They are in the Validation stage, and you are in the Justify stage.)
- ◆ They are in control of the sale and you are just doing what you are told to do.

None of these options seems to be a good choice, but salespeople consistently find themselves in these dilemmas. Why? It's because salespeople do not fully understand the Validate step. The prospect needs to *take ownership*. You do the same when you buy. Here are some examples.

- ◆ **Shoes:** Most people would never buy a pair of shoes without trying them on. *"Well, I have to see if they fit."* Why do stores spend so much money on those floor mirrors? People have to see what they look like in these shoes, as well as what other people will see when they look at them. Then they also have a discussion with the salesperson on how these shoes would look with other clothes. The buyer has started the process of taking ownership of the shoes.

- ◆ **Software:** Did you ever wonder why software companies spend so much money on packaging? They show screen shots of the actual product, especially games. They are trying to get the user to experience the actual software. They are trying to create a visual transfer of ownership.

- ◆ **Cars:** The test drive has become a standard.

- ◆ **Televisions:** Try to buy a TV without trying out the remote control. Retail stores sell more TVs when they attach the remote control to the TV, which is why you see so many remote controls in all the TV stores.

- ◆ **Computers:** Computer stores display all the latest computers, and you have to try it out before you buy it. You see a computer monitor, mouse, keyboard, and preloaded software—all the same equipment you already have. The computers that are lined up at the store are basically all the same, but you still have to try out the one you want to buy; see if you can buy a computer without going up to one and trying it out.

  What are you actually doing when you are trying out a computer? You're not *learning* anything. You're *transferring ownership*.

Prospects are not educating themselves at this point in the Buy/Sell process. They are *validating their educational experience*. This is what prospects need to do at this point, and what salespeople need to learn about and control. The preceding examples are easy ones, but you can give an example of any product and service, and it would still hold true.

It's Validation, Not Education!

In this phase of the Buy/Sell cycle, prospects want to transfer ownership of the proposed solution to their needs. They need to digest fully the entire picture. The brain is filtering information and creating a picture so the prospect understands what is being offered. He or she is not learning anything new at this time; they learned what they needed to learn in the Education phase of the process. Now is the time for prospects to validate their educational experience, to prove to themselves that the shoes fit and look just right, the TV does respond to the remote, and the display samples of the software product do indeed look like something they can handle and use effectively.

Think about the car test-drive. You educated yourself on the car you wanted. You might have spent months learning about this vehicle, or just 10 minutes. Whatever the time frame you used, you did educate yourself about the car. Then you needed to validate your educational experience, so you took the car for a test drive. During that drive, you did not educate yourself. You checked whether the car handled and felt like you expected it to, whether it lived up to your educational experience based on quality, feel, and overall satisfaction. You were validating your educational experience.

Now some of you are saying,

> "Wait, I really do test-drive the car to learn more about the performance or about the overall feel of the car. It's important in my decision, and I'm learning, not validating anything."

You're right. A demonstration of a product or service serves one of two purposes: It can validate an educational experience, or it can educate. But just because it can do one or the other, do not think they are the same. Do not confuse these two processes.

A demonstration can be for educational or for validation purposes. It's all in how you, as a salesperson, set it up. The demonstration of a software product can be used to educate the prospect on the features of the system. The demonstration of a software product can be used to validate the use a prospect has in mind for the system. In the first case, the prospect is learning. In the second, the prospect is validating and taking ownership of something he or she has already learned.

Prospects need Education and Validation (Transfer of Ownership) in two separate steps. Salespeople believe they can Educate and Validate in one step. This just isn't true, and if you try to do it, it will lead to miscommunication between the buyer and the seller.

The act of demonstrating a product or service, from a pair of shoes to an automobile to a multimillion-dollar service implementation, can be in the Education phase or the Validation phase. You need to make sure you do both and do them in two different steps, even if it is in the same meeting.

- ◆ **"We had a great demo. We showed them what we wanted them to see, and we performed flawlessly."** This is Education, not Validation.

- ◆ **"We had a great demo. We showed them what they asked to see and then went into the conference room and discussed at length how they're going to use it."** This is Validation, after an Educate step. Two different steps are taking place in the same meeting, which is fine.

- ◆ **"I was telling them exactly what we do. I know they got it. They were asking great questions about what we do and what our plans are for the future. After lunch, they diagrammed out how they're going to use our solution."** This is a good Validate after an Educate step. It's an example of Transfer of Ownership.

The brain has a hard time educating and validating at the same time. When it is in education mode, it is learning. It is receptive, and new information is being acquired. When it's in validation mode, it's doing something very different. It is rationalizing to itself what it has learned. It's asking itself,

"How am I going to use this?"
"Is this the right thing for me?"
"Can this be used for what I want to use it for?"

In the examples above, the demos of the product and discussion of the service was education. Where the prospects asked questions about the product/service being offered, that was education too. Where the prospects asked questions about how they would be using the product/service, or when it would be delivered, then transfer of ownership is starting. When the prospect starts to diagram out specifically how the product/service is going to fit into their current process, then transfer of ownership is really beginning to take hold.

Prospects are now satisfied that they have learned something and understand what it will do for them, usually both for themselves and their company. This is the process of validation or transfer of ownership, and if you think it all happens at the same time, you are in the same boat as many reactive salespeople. ProActive salespeople know that they must educate and validate at different times. It could happen on one sales call, in which after the educational part of the presentation, the salesperson asks the prospect,

> "Now that we have explained what we do, and how you would use it, how do you see this product/service benefiting you and your company?"

This break in thinking for the prospect, from education to figuring out WIIFM, is the difference between Educate and Validate, and the ProActive salesperson would never go from Educate to Justify without Transfer of Ownership, or the Validate step. The temptation to skip a step is very high. The prospect may be anxious for a proposal. The competitive bids may be due the next day. The prospect has told you this is the next step, and you really believe him. These are all valid reasons, but if you make the jump from Educate to Justify, you will lose control of the sale, be on the path headed to Maybeland, and may never figure out why you are not making your quota.

Let the Buyer Drive: ProActively Inducing the Transfer of Ownership

So now that you know the difference between Education and Validation, the question is, How do you get prospects to validate your information so it makes sense to them and, once that happens, continue on the Buy/Sell process in your favor? Maybe that's not what you were thinking exactly, but it's close.

You have two choices. Prospects can come up with the validation by themselves, or you can assist them. You can have the prospect do all the work and hope they come up with a solution that is in your favor, or you can ProActively induce the transfer of ownership. The goal, obviously, is to learn how to keep control of this Buy/Sell cycle, and ProActively induce transfer of ownership. ProActive salespeople know they must sell for themselves, because to give control to the prospect right now will lead you towards Maybeland. So how do you keep control of the sale, have the prospect take ownership of your solution, and learn how to induce transfer of ownership ProActively? Believe it or not, that's the easy part, because this one is all up to you. It is all in how you prepare for it.

How you prepare for a validation process will determine how successfully the prospect takes ownership. The prospect has two choices, to take ownership or not. You must assume the prospect wants a solution to his or her needs, so assume they're going to take ownership of someone's solution. The two choices the prospect has are:

1.   To be in control of the taking ownership process.
2.   To let you have control of their taking ownership process.

Most prospects want control, so the key issue is to get them to choose option 2; to make them trust you with control of the process. You will now learn how to take or keep control during this key part of the sale and ProActively induce transfer of ownership.

Transfer of Ownership Tools

Many tools are available to a salesperson to induce the transfer of ownership:

Client visits	Test drives	Custom demonstrations
Brochures	Pilot programs	Customer referrals
Testimonials	Money-back	White board
Home office visits	guarantees	discussions
Trials	Samples	

The list above is not exhaustive. Salespeople can use all the tools they currently have at their disposal to help the prospect transfer ownership. Yes, these are the same tools a salesperson uses to educate the prospect. But the difference between Educate and Validate, from a selling perspective, is in preparation and how it is set up. How you set up the transfer of ownership step the prospect wants to go through is what makes the difference.

The key to transfer ownership ProActively is to *manage expectations*. You need to get prospects to commit to making a decision before the transfer of ownership takes place. If they see what they want to see, if their expectations (which have already been stated up front) are met, they will commit to a buy. The best transfer of ownership demonstrations happen before the transfer of ownership takes place. You ask questions and have a conversation with the prospect about:

- The education they have already had.
- What it means to them.
- What they would do with the solution if they had it now.

An example:

"Well Mr. Smith, we have had a good series of meetings so far. This morning, we had a demonstration to educate you and your team on the range and depth of our software. Any questions so far?"

"No, not really. I think we have a good understanding of what you can do. I think we are ready for you to send us a proposal, complete with numbers, so we can get a good handle on the costs and implementation schedule."

"Great."

This sounds like a good meeting so far. You've done your homework and are in a good position. You've used a demonstration of the software system to educate the prospect on what the system can really do. You now have two choices. You can jump to a proposal just like the prospect has suggested, or you can ProActively induce transfer of ownership. Here's how it might play out:

Choice 1: *"That sounds like a great idea. Why don't we put a proposal together and I'll personally drop it off to you next Friday."* *"Perfect. We're anxious to get this project going."*

Choice 2: *"That sounds like a great idea, Mr. Smith. We want to make sure our proposal meets your actual requirements. Before we deliver a proposal, we need to discuss the implementation. We've scheduled some time this afternoon to discuss the implementation schedule for this project. Will you or someone from your team be available? To begin, could you describe to us, once a system like this is implemented, what your expectations would be? What would be happening in your organization and in others that would be affected by a new system such as this?"*

Clearly, these are two different approaches. In Choice 1, the client has taken control, the salesperson is following what the client wants, and the salesperson has left the transfer of ownership up to the client. In Choice 2, the salesperson has control and knows that transfer of ownership has yet to be achieved. The salesperson wants to move the prospect to the Transfer of Ownership phase of the buyer's Buy/Sell cycle and does so by asking the prospect to describe what his operation would be like if he had the software up and running right now. The salesperson just used a tool called the TimeDemo^{Tool} to begin the transfer of ownership (see Figure 10-1).

TOOL   **TimeDemo**^{Tool}

For the most part, the brain has no natural way of telling actual time. You have been given frames of reference with which to tell time—seconds, minutes, hours, days, weeks, months, years, and so on—which you use to organize your thoughts, appointments, and your time.

The mind, however, can travel in time. It can go back and remember as well as go forward and imagine. This time-travel capability of the mind is a very powerful tool to be used in transfer of ownership.

Figure 10-1 TimeDemo^{Tool}

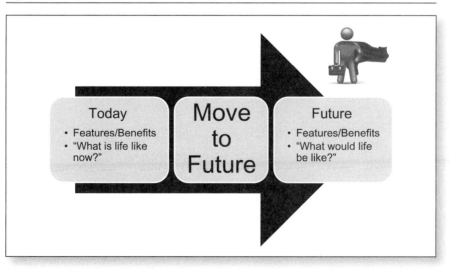

Here is how the TimeDemo™ works. It is a three-step process. You discuss what today's reality is. You then discuss what tomorrow's reality could be. Then you discuss what the prospect would be doing if tomorrow's reality actually happens. These end up being future benefits, which will happen only if the prospect implements your solution.

What do you think these future benefits are? They are the hopes and dreams of the prospect.

> *"Well, if I had this up and running, and everything was working well, I would be able to then take on my next project, which I have been waiting for months to tackle."*

> *"So if I had this TV in my living room right now, I wouldn't have to fight my kids over what I want to watch. I would be able to go to the other room and watch what I wanted to watch for a change."*

> *"If this project is implemented, the return on this investment would fuel our new product development team and give them about a 3-month head start on that new project. I can tell you my president would be really happy about that."*

These future benefits the prospect is dreaming about are now mentally a part of your proposal, since you were the one who had this discussion with the prospect. They will anchor their future benefits to your solution, which becomes a nontransferable competitive benefit for you. Some additional rules about TimeDemos are:

◆ The prospect is going to have this future benefits conversation with someone, so it might as well be you. Prospects need to look out into the future and be comfortable with their fear of the unknown in order to move forward. You need to discuss with them what their life is going to be like once the solution is in place. Moving from Step 2 to Step 3 is critical in a TimeDemo. They need to do that and "see" the future.

◆ The prospect may try to make the benefits generic, more company oriented than personal. For a TimeDemo to work, it must be personal as well as company oriented in nature. Both what's in it for them as an individual as well as what's in it for the company must be addressed.

◆ If the prospect tries to keep their future benefits a secret, you're probably dealing with the wrong person or are in a bad competitive position. Prospects who have decision authority, those who have the biggest stake in the game, are the ones who want to share with—and usually elicit help from—someone with whom they are going to do business.

♦ Time discussions should be visual because 70 percent of the world is visually oriented. They need to "see" the benefits. Make sure you create the mental picture in the prospect's mind. Use charts, graphs, overheads, white boards, and flipcharts. Use these visual tools to make it interactive as well as visual.

♦ Make sure the TimeDemo discussions are in the right language, since the benefits to each level in the prospect's organization are different.

♦ Keep the prospect involved. During the TimeDemo, you should be acting like a conductor, not first violin in the orchestra. Let the prospects assimilate the benefits to them in the future; do not merely tell them and hope they "get it."

What's Your Dressing Room?

My friend Jim tells a story that puts a new twist on the concept of transfer of ownership.

He was a salesperson dealing with Fortune 100 customers. His average deal size was $500,000, and he carried a $4.5 million quota. He knew selling and knew all about completing the transfer of ownership.

He was expounding to his wife, Nancy, on selling and transfer of ownership in a Buy/Sell process, and Nancy commented that transfer-of-ownership selling is the difference between Nordstrom and Macy's. (She had sold for Nordstrom for many years, and had been a Pacesetter, which is the top sales ranking a Nordstrom salesperson can achieve annually.)

Jim discounted her expertise.

"Retail selling is not real selling. There is no real prospecting, sales cycle, or qualification skills in retail sales. Business-to-business selling, where the solution is mutually agreed to, and the value runs into the tens and hundreds of thousands of dollars, is very different," he claimed.

She was adamant in her position.

"I'll take you down to Nordstrom and show you that we solution-sell at Nordstrom, and transfer of ownership is our number one goal. You see, my job at Nordstrom was not to sell people clothes. My job was to get the customer in a position where I had a better than 50 percent chance of winning. If I could do that, I had a good chance of closing the sale."

"How did you get the customer in a better than 50 percent probability of closure situation?" (Jim does tend to go on like this. Don't know how that marriage has survived.)

"Come on down to Nordstrom and see for yourself."

So they went and stopped in where she used to work, in a women's sportswear clothing area. They stayed on the outside perimeter and observed. Within a few minutes, they saw a husband and wife shopping. The wife had a blouse and two pairs of pants, and was shopping for a few more items. Her husband, who was shopping with her, was fidgety, constantly looking at his watch, and clearly not thrilled to be there.

A Nordstrom salesperson approached the couple, and did what Jim thought was one of the dumbest things he had ever seen in sales. She walked up to the wife and instead of saying, *"Can I help you?"* (as most retail store clerks reactively do), she said, *"May I reserve a dressing room for you?"* To Jim's amazement, the wife gave the salesperson the clothes she had on her arm, and the salesperson took them to the back of the department where the dressing rooms were and hung up the clothes in a dressing room.

Jim considered this a selling faux pas, since the buyer at that time didn't have any ownership. She didn't have the clothes in her possession, there was really nothing keeping her in the store, and she was perfectly free to leave. Jim thought this just proved his point, that retail selling is very different than real selling, but all of a sudden, the husband realized his wife didn't have the clothes she had picked out and made his move. *"Honey, I'm sorry you really couldn't find what you were looking for, but we really have to go soon. It's getting late."* She turned to her husband and said, *"We can't go . . . they've reserved a dressing room for me."* She then marched past her husband to the dressing room area to try on her clothes.

A few minutes later, the wife appeared from the dressing room wearing one of the new outfits and paraded in front of her husband. She asked her husband what he thought. Guess what the husband had to say? "You look good in that one." He probably knew that if he said "It's just not you," or "You can do better," that's exactly what she would do, to continue to shop until she found something else. So the husband had two choices, say it looks good and let her decide if she wanted to buy it, or say he didn't like it—and she would continue to shop.

Jim was really enlightened when his wife turned to him and said,

"Do you think the Nordstrom salesperson doesn't know this is what exactly is going to happen? For me, a salesperson's job at Nordstrom is not to sell clothes. Her job is to sell dressing rooms. She knows if she gets the customer to try the clothes on, she has a better than 50 percent chance of closing the sale. Our transfer-of-ownership vehicles are the dressing rooms."

To really pound the story home, she continued: "You see, that's the difference between Nordstrom and Macy's. At Nordstrom, we sell dressing rooms. Our dressing rooms are lively and very well appointed, and you don't mind spending time in them. With so many mirrors and elevated dressing platforms that make you look slimmer, you just have to look good. Also, no one ever thinks to ask for a discount in a dressing room. At Macy's, I wonder sometimes if they even have dressing rooms. The ones they have are not as well laid out or as nice as the ones at Nordstrom. Nordstrom makes the dressing room a part of the sale, where Macy's thinks it is where you go to try on clothes, and lets the buyer go there by themselves, so the salesperson is not really in control of the sale. Since Macy's sells clothes, to get a 10 to 30 percent discount at Macy's is much easier than at Nordstrom. I ask for discounts at Macy's all the time, and I usually get one. At Nordstrom, it is almost impossible to get one."

Transfer of ownership does indeed happen even at the retail sale level. It's all in the setup.

How do you induce transfer of ownership ProActively? How do you make sure you allow the prospect to take ownership and help you in the sales process? What tools could you use right now as transfer of ownership tools rather than just educational tools? What is *your* dressing room?

A final note on the Validate phase: Sometimes, during the process of Transfer of Ownership, the prospect learns something new or thinks of something that has a negative impact on the process. This has certainly happened to me, and it may have happened to you: When this happens, you have three options:

1. **Further Questioning:** Use the Three Levels of Why[Tool] (in Chapter 9) to find out the real objection and overcome it.

2. **More Detail:** What is the real reason something has become important, and can it be addressed by the current solution? Does it have a logical or emotional basis? Usually it is emotional, so probe for fears.

3. **Reeducation:** Go back to the Educate process. You have missed something, and the Buy/Sell process will go no farther until this issue is settled.

Validate is the step in the Buy/Sell process that most salespeople forget. Salespeople are so interested in getting to the next step that it's easy to run right over the prospect's need to complete transfer of ownership. A salesperson hears the prospect say, "I get it," and actually believes he or she does, and goes for the close. The ProActive salesperson knows the difference between a first "I get it" and the second "I get it." (Sound familiar? You're right. We discussed this in Chapter 1, but it's important enough to repeat here.)

The first "I get it" means the prospect understands and his or her education is complete. The prospect got what you have been describing about your product/service. The second "I get it" means he or she not only understands what you are selling, but also how he or she is going to use your solution to improve what he or she is doing and how he or she is going to make money at it. This is a big difference—the ProActive difference.

Homework Assignments

The concept of a homework assignment is straight from the *disqualification* mindset. (We promised we'd get to this, and here we are.) You need to have the prospect put some sweat equity into this deal, or they won't be adding any value and will treat your solution like a commodity, since they never put any work into it.

Have you ever bought a TV or a car for someone else? Did you notice since you did not have any emotional attachment to it, you really did not care if you negotiated too hard, made someone mad, or even didn't get the item you went shopping for? You had no equity into the matter, so why would you care.

Now imagine you are buying the TV for your own personal viewing. Just think of the lengths you go to so you can select the right one. You will listen to the salesperson for hours if they know what they are talking about. If they tell you they need you to do something, you're going to do it, because after all, it's your TV.

As a salesperson, you must realize that serious buyers need to put some sweat equity into the sale. If you believe your job is to do what the customer tells you to do, since if you do what they ask you to do, and you do it well, you will get the order, you're wrong.

Well, there's a tool to help you ensure that the prospect puts in her share of sweat equity, the Gives/Gets[Tool].

TOOL   Gives/Gets[Tool]

You need to come up with Gives and Gets. For everything you Give a prospect, you should Get something in return. Without this mutual relationship, chances are you are going to be treated like a vendor and not a partner. A Get is a homework assignment you ask from the prospect to make sure they have an interest in this process. If they do not want to do simple homework assignments, this is a disqualification issue, and you should consider stopping the Buy/Sell process, since you are probably not in control.

Examples of Gives and Gets are:

Gives	Gets (Prospect's Homework Assignments)
Initial presentation	Validation of agenda
Pre-educate call	Company background information sent
Education presentation	Background of attendees and interests
Demonstration	Sample data
Detailed proposal	Red-lined markup of this draft
Final proposal	Russian in attendance

Use these homework assignments, and think of others, to allow for transfer of ownership of the solution one step at a time, to disqualify as quickly as you can, and to be ProActive in the Buy/Sell process.

If Validate is the step most people skip, Justify is the step where more salespeople lose control of the sale than in any other step in the process. Let's go take a look.

CHAPTER 11

Justify

NOW THE PROSPECT HAS TAKEN A BIG STEP. They understand what you are offering, and they have taken ownership of it. The prospect is moving along a path to make a decision. They make a stop before they are willing to commit, however, at Justify.

The Justify part of the process is where the prospect needs to rationalize the decision they are going to be making. It's when you go out and look at the car once more before you buy it. You drive by the house you are ready to make an offer on one last time to be sure you haven't overlooked anything. The prospect asks for one more demonstration, has one last set of questions, or needs to have a top-level overview before he or she can continue.

Many things happen in the Justify phase. The prospect is having second thoughts, or is trying to rationalize the purchase, or is putting a final evaluation on the risks and the ROI analysis. The prospect is in the home stretch, and the one thing that will keep you on the path of getting this sale is to maintain control of the process.

Reasons for Justification: Institutional and Individual

Prospects will always have two sets of reasons for their decision in a sale. There are the Institutional reasons and the Individual reasons. The ProActive salesperson makes sure they have both of these reasons identified and addressed for every sale. The Institutional reason is one that has its focus on the company or the institution.

Typical Institutional Reasons

Return on investment	Increase competitiveness
Return on assets	Less risk to the business
Decrease overhead	Strategic advantage
Increase revenue	Product diversification

These reasons center around advantages the company will receive if the solution you are offering is implemented.

Individual reasons are ones that benefit the prospect or members of the prospect's team personally. There is an advantage in the solution for them, personally. Individual wins focus on WIIFM. Individual reasons have a personal slant and are usually very emotionally based. They are very dominant in the decision process.

Typical Individual Reasons

Gets the boss off my back.	Enables me to implement something I have always been interested in.
Puts me in line for a promotion.	
Is tied to executive compensation.	Gives me more power in the company.
Frees up my time for other things.	
Allows me to do more of what I really want to do.	Gives me my weekends back so I can spend time with the kids.

Which reason, Individual or Institutional, do you think shows up in company ROI documents? Which one do you think is the real reason why people make decisions? The important thing is that a ProActive salesperson knows *both* for every deal. Just having one without the other leaves you vulnerable. It gives the competition an opening to exploit. A reactive salesperson usually knows one or the other, and is usually happy with it.

> *"The reason they want to buy from us is that it will lower their cost."*
>
> *"Jim wants this solution. He has been looking forward to this project for months. It will finally give him the credibility he has been looking for."*
>
> *"The company needs this for their expansion."*

It's easy to pick out the Individual and the Institutional reasons. Make sure you have them both, and do not get lulled into thinking that one is sufficient. You need Institutional reasons to help the prospect develop an ROI document and to have discussions with upper-level managers (those Russians and Greeks again). You need to have Individual reasons because most if not all decisions are emotional, as we know from using our Three Levels of Why^{Tool}.

Helping the Customer Justify

There are four tools in this chapter that will help you to get the prospect to make a decision, which salespeople call the close. The goal for the ProActive salesperson in the Justify phase is to overcome any last-minute objections, work with the prospect to ensure that you are in the best competitive position possible, and SBP the sale to the last phase of the Buy/Sell process. The ProActive tools for Justify are:

- ♦ Implementation Plan^{Tool}
- ♦ Drop/Push/Pull^{Tool}
- ♦ CliffDive^{Tool}
- ♦ SST—Short-Term Transfer^{Tool}

Let's look at them one at a time.

TOOL | **The Implementation Plan^{Tool}**

It's now, during the Justify phase, that the prospect may start to get a bit nervous.

> *"Is this expenditure the right one?"*

"Do we need to look at other vendors?"

"Is this really the right time to make an investment like this?"

The pressure for a prospect to stray from a SalesMap can get very strong. You can keep the prospect in line and on track with an Implementation Plan.

You know the importance of the prospect's Implementation Date (I-Date), and you know that Buyers Buy Backwards (BBB). With this information, you developed a SalesMap that you've been working on since Educate. You and the prospect are now in the Justify phase of the Buy/Sell process, you are getting close to decision time, and closing in on the time when prospects need to sign an order so they can meet their Implementation Date. To make sure you are in control and can validate your control of the process within all levels in the organization, you need to develop an Implementation Plan.

Most selling organizations are focused on selling a product or service, as well as making sure that the prospect, who once they have purchased is no longer a prospect but is a buyer and a customer, fully utilizes the product or services that are being sold. To do that, most selling organizations agree that the first 30 to 90 days after the buyer's Implementation Date are very critical. This first 30 to 90 days or so is the time when the buyer starts using the solution he has purchased and begins a customer relationship with your company.

If customers work hard to use the goods/service they have purchased from you in the first 30 to 90 days after implementation, it goes a long way in determining how satisfied the buying and selling organizations are going to be. The customers who do a great job of planning and spending time in the first 30 to 90 days, really stretching the solution they have purchased, end up being the most satisfied customers. It's very important, then, that prospects have a plan of action for those first 30 to 90 days after they take delivery. You now need to develop an Implementation Plan to help the buyer through those first 30 to 90 days. You need to develop it not only for the sake of a satisfied customer, but also for you to win the sale. So, exactly what is this Implementation Plan, or I-Plan?

The I-Plan tool is a one-page document, typically written in value-based language (Russian), to help the upper management of the buying organization determine whether it is effectively using its resources as well as using you, the selling organization, to achieve its maximum return on the investment in the quickest amount of time (see Figure 11-1). The I-Plan outlines the top three to five (or more) areas that management of the buying organization should focus on internally to make sure its implementation team is doing its job effectively. You have gathered this information by working with individuals in the prospect's organization and by referencing successful implementations of your product or service with previous customers. You are giving the management of the buying organization a list of items that they need to oversee to ensure their people are going to do their job well. Senior management is always looking for a map of what measurable objectives it should focus on to maintain top performance in its organization, and you have taken some of the guesswork (and therefore some of the risk) out of it.

In addition, your I-Plan includes the three to five or so objectives that the customer management team should hold you, the vendor, to. Your prospect's management is spending a lot of resources on you and your organization. They want a return on this investment, and they want the return to have low risk and yield a maximized amount of money in the shortest amount of time. By giving the buying management a list of objectives it needs to hold you to, you are helping them to accomplish these goals.

Many organizations have implementation plans that are assembled after the purchase has been made. It is a customer service document that companies work on with their customers to implement the solution at the user level. How does your ProActive I-Plan differ from other user-centric implementation plans?

Figure 11-1 Implementation Plan

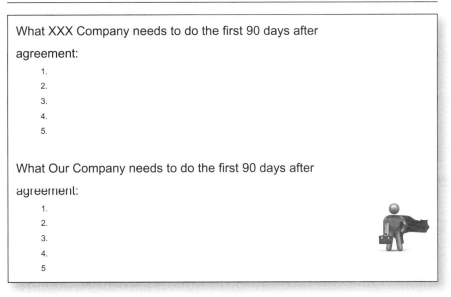

What XXX Company needs to do the first 90 days after agreement:

1.
2.
3.
4.
5.

What Our Company needs to do the first 90 days after agreement:

1.
2.
3.
4.
5

- ◆ **An I-Plan is a selling document.** It is used during the sales process, not after. It should be used to assess your position in the sale and help determine your competitive position and your next step.

- ◆ **An I-Plan is written in Russian.** You use it to get back in to see the vice president. You've been working with all languages, and you need to make sure the top executive in the process is on board. Even if you are being blocked by a manager (Spaniard), you can use an I-Plan to get back up to the decision maker, since it is written in value-based language, and for 15 or 20 minutes of their time, you are going to maximize their investment and lower their risk. The only Russian who wouldn't give you 15 or 20 minutes of their time is one who isn't planning to buy from you.

- ◆ **An I-Plan is used to help managers look good.** If your manager or user is an up and comer in the organization, they will appreciate an I-Plan because it shows they were thorough, prepared, and had a strategic rather than just a tactical look at the project. It makes them look good to their boss and also makes the boss look good to the organization.

- ◆ **An I-Plan is a mutually beneficial document for transfer of ownership.** It shows prospects their risks and what they should keep an eye on to minimize those risks, since risks can cost money. It helps you because it gives you insight into what is important to the senior executive and lets you assess how serious they are regarding your solution.

- ◆ **An I-Plan can be used in the final closing step to ask for an order.** As part of your proposal, it can be used to show your professionalism and thoroughness. It can incorporate the Implementation Date, which combined with your SalesMap lets you control the Buy/Sell process to which the prospect has already committed.

The I-Plan is a sales document positioned in between Validate and the final proposal that gives you information at a key juncture in the Buy/Sell process. It lets you test out the process you have gone through already, allows you access to senior managers to get their buy-in, and sets the stage for you to control the outcome of the final proposal.

A FINAL NOTE: The I-Plan and SalesMap are two of the most powerful tools in this book, but we have observed that, of the salespeople who have been through ProActive Selling, fewer than 30 percent actually implement these two tools. Why? The reason is they take some work. Unlike the Flip or Three Levels of Why tools, they require some actual preplanning and detailed work. Like anything else, the things that take the most time usually yield the biggest rewards. Use these tools!

Let's move to the next tool that is very useful at this stage of the Buy/Sell process, the Drop/Push/Pull^{Tool}.

TOOL | **Drop/Push/Pull**^{Tool}

It's now decision time, and the decision is yours to make. You've gotten to this stage by following a process, and with skills and tactics, you've put yourself in a strong sales position. If you feel you are in a strong position, one where you believe you have a better than 50 percent chance of winning, you should SBP to the next step called Close. If you don't think you are in the best competitive position, you have three choices. You can:

1. Drop it. Any more time or effort by you is just throwing good resources after a bad situation.

2. Push to a Close. Pushing is not the most desirable option, but owing to time constraints, competitive pressure, or the prospect wanting to make a decision ASAP, you may have to push. When you push you are out of control, so it usually costs you something, and that something will cost you money. You'll end up discounting, matching a competitive offering, or giving something away to get the order. Whatever it is, pushing a deal is risky, doesn't ensure a victory, and in the long and short run, costs you margin.

3. Pull. The third option is to go back and start pulling. Go back to the Educate process and start again to pull the prospect through the Buy/Sell process and create the value for your product or service. Going back through the Educate/Validate/Justify process is different for every sale. In some cases, it may take five minutes. In others, it may take five hours, five meetings, five days, five weeks, or five months. The point is, you have to go back and get control of the Buy/Sell process. If the prospects don't understand your solution and take ownership of it, they're not going to understand your price. If they don't understand your price, you have violated the Law of Value Creation.

THE LAW OF VALUE CREATION

If all things are equal, people will buy on price. The job of a ProActive salesperson is to create a value difference so prospects do not see things as equal, because they are not.

ProActive salespeople know that if all things are equal, and the prospect is deciding based on price, they have not done their job.

Your best chance to finalize this sale is to stay the course. Stay with the strategies you started out with and have continued with during the entire process. By staying the course and using the tools described in this chapter, you will put yourself in the position of greatest return, and that return is the order.

Which brings us to the CliffDive^{Tool}.

TOOL | **CliffDive**^{Tool}

You have done a great job. You are near the end of the Buy/Sell process . . . however, you get the sense the buyer may be losing momentum.

Remember, you're asking a prospect to do something they hate doing: You're asking them to change, and people and companies hate to change—even when they know they have to. That's why they're not returning your calls. It's not that they don't want to implement your idea, or to buy your product; they really do. It just seems like it's a big investment, a big step forward, a huge risk. To them, it feels like jumping off a cliff.

This is a time to use a tool that will help you jump off the cliff with them, which is why it's called CliffDive. You'll want to use this tool when you are near the end of the sale, and you think the prospect is getting cold feet. They are not returning your calls and when you do talk to them, they are evasive and noncommittal, with comments such as the following:

"We still have some final things we have to go over."

"There are still a few more people we need to get buy-in from."

"Really, we'll be ready to go ahead next week."

The problem you are facing is fear. Fear is what really drives decisions, either to completion or to delay. Even the fear of not making a decision is a powerful motivator. Lucky for you, fear is in the mind, and you can use that little fact to help prospects overcome their fears.

CliffDive takes some of a prospect's irrational fears and puts them into perspective (see Figure 11-2). The key is to shift the focus of prospects from today to the future. Today is terrifying for prospects because today is when they have to make the decision. It's the point of no return. A decision has to be made, and it better be a right, good, and fair one. It better be a great, profitable, and correct decision, one that can be implemented, measured, and bought into. The pressure is intense . . . no wonder prospects hesitate.

Today ⟶ Tomorrow

However, if "today" is terrifying, "tomorrow" is a different story. That's the secret of the CliffDive tool: It takes prospects to tomorrow, and beyond. Let's say tomorrow is 30 to 60 days out. Ask the prospect to imagine that they have implemented your solution, started using the item they purchased from you or began to put into operation the product/service you are offering, and it was doing very well. Now ask them, how would they feel?

How would they feel if it was 30 to 60 days from now, and the investment they made has done everything it was expected to do? Their response would likely be:

"Well, I'd feel great."

"I'd feel relieved."

"It would be really good."

Those small sentences, those few words of feelings, are like a digital picture capturing a moment in time—but a time that is different than Today. You're successfully moving the prospect away from all the decision-making fears of Today, and focusing him or her on the feelings of Tomorrow, which are great feelings. The more the prospect thinks and discusses those feelings, the less the fears of Today will rear their ugly heads.

Don't stop now. You have moved the prospect to the edge of the cliff. Now, have the prospect jump off the cliff (see Figure 11-2), which will land them in a great place, about 3 to 6 months out, called NEXT.

Figure 11-2 CliffDive^{Tool}

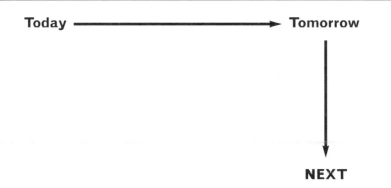

NEXT is where prospects want to be, where their hopes, dreams, and desires are realized. The decision to buy, which seemed so daunting when viewed from the present, is long gone. From the viewpoint of NEXT, and all the great things happening in the 3-to-6-month time frame of NEXT, the decision to buy was just one step in the right direction. CliffDive lowers prospects' fears, and minimizes risk, by making the decision just one step in the process that will lead to success in the future.

A SPECIAL NOTE OF CAUTION: CliffDive only works with Russians, that is, decision makers. Decision makers have the vision and the strategy in place to see what's next. Managers (Spaniards) are waiting to be told what to do; if you ask them what's next, they really can't tell you, because they haven't been told themselves yet. Use the CliffDive tool at the decision maker's desk, and the results will be a shorter sales cycle. Prospects want and need to change. They just need some help jumping off that cliff.

We have one more ProActive tool for you to use at the Justify stage, the STT—Short-Term Transfer^{Tool} (see Figure 11-3).

TOOL STT—Short-Term Transfer^{Tool}

You should use the STT tool when someone in the prospect organization becomes stuck and cannot complete their buying decision. It helps them effortlessly accept the transfer of ownership by focusing on the time period immediately after the purchase.

Much has been said about the I-Date, the date that prospects are going to use the solution you are providing. However, if you time-travel them to immediately *after* they make their decision, it may unjam the decision roadblock. (If this tool reminds you of the TimeDemo^{Tool} from

Figure 11-3 STT—Short-Term Transfer^{Tool}

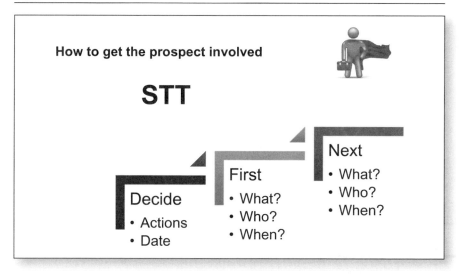

Chapter 10, it should. They are similar, but this one is much more immediate, right here, right now, tomorrow, or next week—not in 6 months or a year from now when the new system is installed.)

I bought a car for my daughter the other day. Sometimes when I make a purchase, I think about why I decided to buy. Of course, I try to relate the process to some ProActive sales tools.

I thought about the reasons I decided to buy a used Toyota for my daughter. Why did I purchase it?

♦ It was in my price range. A few dollars more, but within the range.

♦ It had all the features I wanted.

♦ It was in good mechanical shape. A dealer checked it out.

♦ I needed it now. The other option was having my daughter drive my car, which, after my son put a major dent in it a few years earlier, was not going to happen.

♦ I had spent enough time looking and was ready to make a decision.

Time, Risk, ROI, Brand, Leverage—all the elements of ValueStar are on that list of reasons. Cause and Effect is covered as well. So, what pushed me over the edge?

Here's what was *not* a deciding factor: *"Mr. Miller, this car will last your daughter at least 5+ years."*

That was true of every car, so why did the dealer use this? Probably because it sounded good and he had used it hundreds of times before—in other words, it was a success pattern (remember these, from Chapter 2?). What a waste of a good sales effort.

The salesman's following line of questioning, however, was unique:

"So Mr. Miller, when did you plan on giving it to her? Where will your first drive be? Will you put a big red bow on it when you give it to her?"

I had to think about these questions, and the more I thought about them, the more Transfer of Ownership I had . . .

"I'll get the bow on the way home at the Party Store off Saratoga Ave. I'm sure they have one, and it's on the way. Our first drive, heck, we were all planning to go out to dinner tonight, so she can drive us in her new car. Since today is Friday, this is a great day to give it to her, since I don't want to waste another weekend looking at cars."

What happened was STT—Short-Term Transfer. I had already validated the long-term buy-in for the car, but wasn't motivated to get started. I didn't have a clear idea what I was going to do first (or second or third) after buying the car. What were the baby steps I was going to take once I had made this decision?

For me, knowing those baby steps that I was going to take in the very short term—that day, those first few hours after I made the decision—made me make a decision on the spot.

What are your prospects doing in the short term (the first 1 to 10 days) after their decision? Usually, they have no idea how they're going to get started. If they can't respond, give them some hints, best practices, or suggestions. Even if you gave them the hint, it has to become *their* idea. They have to put some sweat equity into the process. Thinking what to do first should take the pressure off "the Decision" itself and get them back to thinking about the process (good), not the event (bad). If they cannot think of what happens in the short term after the buy, there's no transfer of ownership, no urgency . . . and no deal.

CHAPTER 12

The Skill of Closing the Deal

YOU'VE DONE IT. You've walked with the prospect through the Buy/Sell process, and you feel you're in the best competitive position you can be in. You've worked together with the prospect to develop a hard-hitting proposal, complete with an Implementation Plan and a SalesMap of all the activities you've done with them throughout the Buy/Sell process. Now you're ready to proceed to the final step.

What Is a Close?

"The close" means something different to a prospect than it does to a salesperson. To a prospect, it is the final logical step in a business evaluation process. Prospects and their team have been involved every step of the way through an evaluation that will require an investment of resources to change a process within the organization. Or, they also may be purchasing goods or service by themselves, and the need for a committee and a process may be minimal. In this case, the prospect has evaluated the need to invest resources, their own money, to change something: the car they drive, their appearance, the place they live, or where they will go on a vacation. Whatever the size or scope of the effort, the prospect sees this step as a *decision*, either yes or no. That's why it's called Decide on the Buyer side of the Buy/Sell process—the prospect is now ready to make a decision.

A reactive salesperson views this step as the time to "close a deal." It's time to get ink on paper, bring it home, get a signature, a John or Jane Hancock, or whatever else you call getting the prospect to commit to your solution. A reactive salesperson sees this as time to get the order, chalk it up in the win column, and get paid. This is one-dimensional thinking.

The obvious problem is that the prospect and the salesperson are going into the final step with different agendas. With two different agendas, there is bound to be some confusion, and there are two different potential outcomes. The ProActive salesperson, however, sees this final step just as the prospect sees it—a chance to make a decision. However, the prospect, in the eyes of the salesperson, has three choices, not two. The prospect can say yes, no, or maybe, where a maybe is anything that prevents a yes or no decision. A maybe could be competition, a delay, a move to table the decision to a higher source—anything that prevents a yes or no. Maybes are never good for a salesperson, since by definition, a maybe means the salesperson is not in control of the process.

So how can a salesperson control the final step? Just like in all the other steps. Control the process, and think like a buyer.

Defining the Process

The art of closing can fill another book by itself. There are numerous negotiating tactics you can use in a sale that is in the closing phase to try to get an order.

- **Good Cop, Bad Cop:** One person takes the side of the customer and is very empathetic, and the other person is the "bad cop" and plays someone who is very hard to deal with.
- **Split the Difference:** The two sides in the negotiation are a set difference apart, and you agree to split the difference.
- **Nibbling:** Offer small increments of something. Give the customer a discount, then offer no sales tax, then give free delivery, then gift wrap it for free, and so on.
- **Agree, Deflect, Agree:** This is a tactic to move someone to a new position. *"I agree with you Mr. Jones. Some people would also think this way, which I'm sure you would agree would . . ."*

- ◆ **Puppy Dog:** Take something and try it out. Like a puppy, once you get it "home," the odds of a return are minimal.
- ◆ **Written Word:** Once something is in writing, it's hard to argue. Think when you shop for something at the shopping mall. Once something has a price tag on it, you rarely think of negotiating from that asking price.

There are many, many more negotiating tactics you can use in a closing situation to try to get the order. By using ProActive selling techniques, you've already done all the hard work by controlling the process. It's now up to you to have the buyer make a yes or no decision, and you do this by working the process you have used already to get the sale to this point—and by thinking like a buyer.

Use the Tools

You have many tools at your disposal that you can use to Summarize, Bridge, and Pull this final meeting to a decision.

The 30-Second Speech^{Tool}

Start the meeting out with a 30-Second Speech: Second Call and Beyond^{Tool}. You remember: Introduction, three discussion points from the last meeting or the entire Buy/Sell process, three final issues or points, suggest the outcome of the meeting, gain agreement, then get into the agenda of the meeting.

30-Second Speech

"Good afternoon, and thank you for attending today's meeting. We've gone through a process over the last few months, and together we've determined that:

1. *The need for a solution in this area is critical. We've documented the steps both of us have taken during this evaluation and arrived at the solution we're going to review today.*

2. *The solution we are offering seems to do exactly what you want.*

3. The budget for this expenditure has already been justified.

> You also stated that you:
>
> 1. *Need this solution immediately,*
> 2. *Are concerned about the delivery and ramp-up time, since you want it up and running by the 22nd of the month, and*
> 3. *You wanted to have two financial options presented to you at this meeting.*
>
> This is what we are here to talk about today, and if we have a successful meeting, we can get a two-day head start by executing the agreement that is in the proposal today, or we can execute the agreement by Friday, as planned to meet your Implementation Date of the 22nd. Is this your understanding of the meeting today?"

This is a 30-Second Speech to begin a Closing meeting. Other tools you will be using in this Closing meeting include the following:

- Implementation Date[Tool]
- SalesMap[Tool]
- Three Languages[Tool]
- Three Levels of Why[Tool]
- Flip[Tool]
- Summarize, Bridge, Pull[Tool]

Implementation Date

In the above example, you already know the prospect wants to have your solution up and running by the 22nd. The focus of the salesperson must be on what is important to the prospect, the Implementation Date and BBB, not the date of the signing of the contract.

SalesMap

Your SalesMap is in the proposal so prospects can remind themselves how much work they have done to get to where they are now. It helps overcome their fears.

"Have we done enough homework so we are comfortable with this change?"

"Are we sure this is the best investment of our resources?"

"Are we sure we can do this in the time required?"

This is the process you and the prospect have gone through together, and it's a competitive advantage because you are probably the only vendor who has created a SalesMap with them.

Implementation Plan

This is also in your proposal, so the fear of the unknown is lessened. The SalesMap looks backward, and the I-Plan looks forward. Both of these tools will lower the prospect's perceived risk of change. The I-Plan shows the prospect what they should be doing in the first 30 to 90 days to maximize their return and improve the overall chance of success, which lessens their fear of the unknown.

The Three Languages

You will probably have managers (Spaniards), vice presidents (Russians), and even a president or CEO (Greek) in your final presentation. Remember to speak all languages, and when in doubt, always speak to a higher language; always speak up.

Three Levels of Why and Flipping

There probably will be some final questions. By now you know the most *in*effective thing you can do is to answer these questions. Your job is not to answer questions first presented to you. Two rules of thumb are:

1. Senior executives ask a question only when they have a good idea of an answer.
2. Your job is to get the real question/answer out, and you do that with Three Levels of Why, and then Flipping.

Summarize, Bridge, and Pull

Summarize, Bridge, and Pull to the final step, and ask for the commitment and decision to start the process together. Make sure you emphasize the dragons. Satisfying these dragons is why they will make a decision.

Stay with this process, and use all the tools to start the meeting, run the meeting, and end the meeting in control of the process. Control the process, and you'll win the sale. Prospects may try to wrestle control from you at the end of the final meeting by delaying making a decision on the agreed-to date. They may stall by deferring to another person not in the meeting or by introducing you to a new time schedule of which you were unaware. You still have your SBP tool, so you can get final control of the meeting, and adjust to any unforeseen circumstances or objections.

Using SBP to Regain Control: Two Examples

Example 1: The prospect has changed the decision date.

> "Well, it seems we've had a good meeting. You've stated your desire to move ahead with the project. You still need it up by the 22nd. Your manufacturing line needs to start on the 25th, or you will have heavy penalties to pay based on commitments you have made to your customers (Dragon). *You cannot make a decision until Monday now, instead of this Friday, since the president will not be back in the office until then. You also said you have talked with him this week and expect no objections.*
>
> We've called our office and found out that if you commit on Monday, we can get everything ready and express ship to make your 22nd date. Do you agree this is where we are?"
>
> "Yes I do."
>
> "Great, so we will be back here on Monday at 10:00 A.M. *to finalize everything so we can make that date of the 22nd.*" (Not "to pick up the order"!)

Example 2: The prospects are nervous about the investment, and want to wait.

> "We've had a good meeting today. You've stated your desire to go ahead with this service, but now want to put it on hold. You're comfortable with the solution, and the investment you are making relative to the return you are getting is well within the realm of acceptability, over $1 million within the first 12 months. You also wanted to make sure the project gets completed within 150 days from commencement of the project, which according to the I-Plan, both sides can commit to.

Based upon the SalesMap and the I-Plan we have worked together on, your risks of this project delivering its proposed financial benefits of over $4 million over 3 years have been identified, and according to you, are acceptable (Dragon). *We have stated our desire to move ahead and meet your schedule, so I think we have had a good meeting, is this correct?"*

"Yes, it has been a good meeting."

"Good. The next step is to look at the financial investment being made. If we can't agree to terms now, the risk increases, as will the time to a solution. We need to figure out what we can do as a team to make this "hold" go away. Is this where we need to go as a next step?"

Just as with a price objection, you have to summarize the Buy/Sell process and the tools you have used, and attack ROI, time, and risk. If you let all things become equal, you need to go back and reeducate. If that still does not work, you are probably dealing with a manager who isn't the final decision maker. The only reason you would still be in a price situation is that you are out of control of the process. Drop, Push, or Pull (see Chapter 11); it's your choice.

The Real Art of Closing Is in the Definition: Think Like a Buyer

The single most important thing in the closing meeting is to *think like a buyer*. In real-life situations, as well as the role-plays students go through in our classes, it's amazing how they get greedy at the end of the sale, think like a salesperson, and ask for the contract to be signed. But it's not about *you*; it's about *them, them, them*. Stay in the prospect's perspective, and close the sale by keeping the perspective on them. Remember the differences between thinking like a buyer and thinking like a seller:

Seller	Buyer
Contract signed	Implementation date
Cost	Return on investment
Price	Investment to get the return desired
Next step forward	Logical decision step
Ask for the order	Make a decision—yes or no
Get contract by end of the month	Make a decision—implementation may be at risk

If you maintain your composure and stay the course of thinking like a buyer, you have the best opportunity to stay in control of this sale.

Celebrate Success

Finally, make sure you celebrate success with your new customer. You have done everything right and worked the tools in *ProActive Selling* to keep in control of the Buy/Sell process. ProActive salespeople make sure they:

1. Tell the buyers they did the right thing.
2. Express to them how pleased you are to have them as a customer.
3. Say when they can expect to hear from you next (SBP).
4. Wrap up professionally.
5. Don't oversell. ProActive salespeople take the order and leave.

Congratulations. You've followed the process, used all the right tools, and are a ProActive salesperson. You've made it through the process of a ProActive sale, and you're thinking of how to use the tools and follow the process on all your prospects. *ProActive Selling* will improve your chances of getting a sale, increase the qualification skills you possess, and give you more tools for you to use at the point of attack, the sales call, than you ever had before.

CHAPTER 13

Using Technology to Sell

NEW TECHNOLOGIES in the past few years have significantly changed the way you are selling today—and technology-led productivity and sales enablement advances are likely to continue in the future.

Here are some of the trends you should be following:

1. **Lead Generation:** Lead generation tactics today include some benefit to the prospect, which is the way to get their attention. These benefits include:
   a. Newsletters
   b. Video e-mails
   c. References
   d. Attached marketing
   e. Website chats
   f. Links

   There are numerous ways you as an individual sales person can use the Web to generate leads.

2. **Video Selling:** If you can iChat with your kids, why don't you iChat with your customers? Salespeople are discovering the advantages of video calls on Skype, Apple, AOL, and Google. Avatar discussion groups such as VenueGen are becoming more and more common.

3. **Cloud Presentations:** The cloud is a technology that has overriding benefits to sales organizations and salespeople. As an individual salesperson, are you organizing your customers and your internal resources? Do you have a discussion group set up with your current customers? Can you get your internal resources to post items to the cloud, giving you immediate access and ensuring that you will have the right presentation at the right time? Are you helping to find solutions for your customers' issues using cloud-based resources?

4. **Apple:** Apple products, including iCloud, iPhone, iChat, and iPad, are on a roll, and you may want to get on that bandwagon. Start by getting a Mac for your home and exploring the possibilities.

5. **Mobile:** You should always be current with mobile technology, whether it's apps, messaging, texting, or even just time management skills. Logging your sales calls on your mobile device is becoming more and more common. Sales technologies are always changing, and they seem to change right when you get comfortable with the application or device you bought last year. Top sales performers are investing their own money to stay ahead of the technology curve, and you should, too.

Sales Touches

Measuring your sales activities by the number of sales calls is a thing of the past. Sales touches—connecting with the prospect through technologies such as e-mail and texts—are now the norm.

Of course, a face-to-face call with a prospect still has more value than an e-mail, and a thirty-minute phone call will have more value than a text message. Sales calls will not go away. However, sales touches can be a positive way to keep the Buy/Sell process moving and can shorten the process altogether. Remember the Law of 2X states that there are two ways of shortening sales cycles.

1. Have shorter meetings.
2. Reduce the time in between meetings.

Sales touches allow you to achieve the second item on that list. Proposing a next step, even if it's a sales touch, by "this Thursday" instead of "next week," will keep your sales moving and, overall, shorten the amount of time it takes to close a sale.

Sales touches include:

♦ Text messages
♦ E-mails
♦ Reference calls
♦ Homework on the Internet
♦ LinkedIn searches and referrals
♦ Reviews of agendas
♦ Pre-reviews of demonstrations
♦ Discussions before the presentations of goals and objectives
♦ Technical conversations with the support group
♦ Having your boss and the prospect's boss meet

As you prepare, think not just about what to do during sales calls, but about the kind of sales touches you can have between calls. The more touches, the more the prospect is working with you to come to a decision point.

Social Media: Getting Involved

It's absolutely surprising to me how many salespeople *don't* use social media. Don't be one of them. Here's how to put together a social media plan that will support your sales efforts.

What Is Your Goal?

Social media is not the ends, but the means. To use social media is not a goal in itself, but a way to achieve specific goals. Thus, the first step in a social media plan is to decide just what you expect to achieve through these new technologies. Here are some typical social media sales goals:

- Generate leads.
- Go broad and deep in current customer base.
- Reach five sales above the quota.
- Create a network of X number of people.
- Educate current customers of specials.
- Sales touch with decision makers monthly.
- Have customers stay in your network for referrals and references.
- Have internal resources stay in touch with you.

Before you pick an effective and realistic goal for social media, there are some questions you'll need to answer first:

- How are your customers online? Do they just have e-mail? Do they use mobile extensively? What percent of your prospects are behind a firewall and unreachable?
- If you start a blog, will you and your customers keep it current? Is this something they do now, or will this be just an idea that sounds good but dies from neglect?
- What benefit will you offer prospects and customers through your use of social media?
- What results will you measure so you know how to improve your efforts over time?

This is not the time to "shoot, then aim," or to jump on a bandwagon. You do want to join the social media trend, but only after you've developed a goal and a strategy.

Beginning Baby Steps

To do your homework and get the answers you need, start by talking with current top salespeople you know, and of course to your current customers. You'll discover that different people tend to use different social media, be it vlogs, blogs, following, tags, SEO, SEM, iChat, podcasts, WebEx meetings, or Twitter. You can bet someone is using something, and as a ProActive salesperson, you need to get up to speed.

Listening is also important. You should implement at least a rudimentary listening platform, such as a NLP or Crucial Conversations.

Finally, build a starting place to hold your conversations. And by this, I mean a social media platform. Here are some key questions that will help you develop the best platform for you:

- What is the best and most effective mix my customers want to hear from me?

- What is current in my industry and what direction is it heading? Some industries are all on Gmail, and some are all Apple users, for instance.

- What do you plan on sharing and providing that will be of value to your customers? People will respond when there is something in it for them.

- Divide the sales process into three areas; leads, work-in-process, and sales. What do you want your strategy to do? Generate leads in new companies? Current companies? Move your sales process along faster? Global account coordination? Do you just want to post items and have customers self-serve and you are generating revenue? Have a definitive goal in mind on what you want your strategy to achieve relative to the Buy/Sell process.

- Can you create links with others so if people hit their site, they have an opportunity to hit yours? This can be done on a person level (be a reference for someone on LinkedIn), or at a company level on their website. Be a reference quote for your customers.

You can build your own brand awareness, and the brand awareness of your companies as well, by executing a good personal social media strategy.

Technology Trends

It's all about execution. Hardware is getting faster, software is getting easier and more intuitive, and networking is everywhere. However, technology trends ebb and flow: What's hot today is yesterday's news tomorrow. How can you stay on top of the technology curve and know what is really productive and not just the latest fad? Here are some of the technology trends that are most relevant to salespeople:

- Mobile
- Video

- Cloud
- Lead generation
- Networking (social media)
- Contact management
- Deal management
- Apps

Don't be afraid of making an investment in software or hardware. You're not losing your money or your time, even if the technology eventually becomes obsolete. I now use an iPhone instead of the Blackberry I used before, but that doesn't mean I didn't get my money's worth out of the Blackberry. Investing a website for yourself is definitely worth the trouble. Your customers can stay in touch with you, look up specials, or explore what they can do with the new products you are announcing. Don't make them wait for you to call them.

Also, work up a blog so your customers can talk to each other. Have a monthly WebEx so your customers can stay in touch with your latest offerings and services (Spaniards will eat this up). Start video chatting or have iChat sessions with your customers to have more useful conversations. Any way that you use social media—and remember to be security conscience while you are doing so—will add to your competitive advantage.

CHAPTER 14

Applying the *ProActive Selling* Process

Implementing the New Rules

You've spent most of your time with this book understanding how a buyer buys, thinking like a buyer to learn what tactics to use during a sales call. It's now time to think like a salesperson and ProActively figure out what to do with all this information. It's good to have added more tools to your sales toolbox, but now you're asking: Which one do I use when? How do I begin?

How to Start: Prepare

The first thing you need to do is get organized. While reading this book, like all outstanding salespeople, you've probably already started applying some of the tools to current accounts, especially the ones that are in your Maybeland. You use a ProActive tool for one account, then remember another tool that could be used for another account, and before you know it, you have used a few tools. *"Hooray,"* you think, *"they work."* You then put the tools back on the shelf, never to use them again.

I've found, in my many years of teaching the ProActive selling process, that teaching the tools once is not enough. Over and over, we hear:

> "I learned an awful lot the first time, but the second time through, I really took away so much more."

I wish salespeople could learn completely on the first go around, and they do learn, but repeated exposure to the tools will make salespeople more successful. You have to plan to use the tools first.

Choose no more than three accounts you currently want to go after with your new set of tools. They may be ones that you are working on now, or all new prospects. Focus on those.

Determine where in the process they are. Is the prospect in the Education phase? Has ownership transferred, and are you in Validate? Have you just started, and are you now planning your Initiate call? Plan out your sales call, determine what you want to accomplish, and then use the tools that apply. You need to have all the tools listed and available to you, or you will end up using two or three, and forgetting all the rest. Appendix A, which follows this chapter, has a list of the Proactive Sales Tools for you to photocopy and post in your office. It will remind you which tools are available to you to use at any given time.

The Second Step: Practice

Once you have started reviewing the tools, practice, practice, practice. Most people will start with a 30-Second Speech^Tool or a Summarize, Bridge, and Pull^Tool. Make sure you script out exactly what you want to do, and include the tools. Try to use them exactly as you have learned them here. It is really easy to do an Intro-2–1 30-Second Speech, and you'll feel good that you at least got one done. But stay with the program. A *real* 30-Second Speech is Intro-3–3-Summarize and Flip. It may feel uncomfortable, but the person sitting across the desk or on the other end of the phone will love it. Practice makes perfect.

Design a SalesMap form. What would one actually look like? Use the computer and make up a sample one. Don't use the example in the book since ownership will not transfer. You have to develop your own ("sweat equity," remember?) from scratch.

What would an Implementation Plan look like? What would be useful for your specific sales situation? The sample I-Plan included in the book can be a good start, but, as with the SalesMap, make up your own.

If you're having difficulty, go back to some of your current customers and ask them what was important to them during the first 30 to 90 days after they implemented what you sold them. Most likely, what you thought was important to them and what they were actually measuring were different; they usually are.

The MMM questions are key. Come up with ways you can ask these questions, the earlier in the sales process, the better. All seven questions are important, and Implementation Date is on the top of the list.

The Three Levels of Why^Tool is fun, but you really have to keep digging to get at the third level of why. Sarah Berry, who works for one of our clients, now claims she is so good at Three Levels of Why that, on a recent call, the prospect at the end of the call proclaimed,

> "I have just told you more information than I should have and more information than I have told anyone else. I'm okay with that though because it has crystallized my thinking as well."

This is a win-win if ever there was one.

Use all the tools, but only a few at a time. Change them week by week, adding some and dropping others. The more exposure you have to the tools, the more you will incorporate them into your actual sales toolbox.

Have a support group in your office. Have an early morning meeting once or twice a week to practice the tactics you're planning to use on your next few sales calls. Practice in front of your peers. This is a very hard thing to do, but it's really very important. If you're all alone or work from home, use the phone. Call others so they can critique and offer assistance. Remember, if one of your fellow sales team members asked you for help, you would offer your help in a second. Asking for help is not a sign of weakness; it's one of the toughest things salespeople can do, since they always think they are in control. Ask for help, and you will be amazed at how quickly you incorporate the tools into your daily sales processes.

The Third Step: Implement the Process

Now that you've learned to use the individual tools, it is time to map out the process. Remember to master the tools first, then the process. This does sound a little backwards, because you are probably used to learning the process first, then the tools. Learning how to sell is like learning anything else, one step at a time. When you learned how to play a musical instrument, it was notes first, then the chords. With sports, learning to drive, or learning how to walk, you started one step at a time. Then the bigger issues become manageable. The same is true with ProActive selling; learn the individual tools first.

Once you've started to master the tools, you can look at the process. As you learned in Chapter 1, there's a process in how people buy, and you need to match your steps to the buyers' steps. Begin with your current accounts, and map out for each one where you are in the ProActive selling process. Follow the right process—it's very easy to get lost in a sale. You must stay focused on the Buy/Sell cycle.

There are three types of "process sellers" out there, and being ProActive is going to make you more successful than either of the other two.

- ♦ **Proposal Sellers** think that by skipping the Educate and Validate steps, they are closer to the close of a sale. These are the most confused salespeople since they gear up for selling a proposal. They start with Initiate and get the prospect initially interested. Then they think, since they have an "interested" prospect, they should just sell a proposal. The proposal has all the relevant information in it, and once the prospect "sees" the value solution in the proposal, they should sign right away. Prospects won't. The proposed solution has no value to the prospect, since there has been no education and transfer of ownership of the value as there has been for your solution. Using this process, you will have to discount to match the prospect's "budget" or competitive offers.

- ♦ **Demo Sellers** are busy selling demos. They believe their job is to get the prospect in front of the solution as soon as possible. Once they see this "thing" perform, they will "see" the value and have to buy. Demo sellers go past the education phase so fast, prospects have no opportunity to understand fully what the salesperson is offering. They get it, but do not really get it. They get what your solution is, but do not get WIIFM. The Law of Creating Value says if all things are equal, prospects will buy on price. Selling demos allow the prospect to see all solutions as equal, since they have not had the opportunity to understand your solution fully, and therefore your price difference. With demo selling you again will have to push to make the sale.

- ♦ **ProActive Process Sellers** are the salespeople who know they have to take the selling process one step at a time, since that is how buyers buy. Skipping steps will allow the prospect to gain control, which is not a good thing. The Buy/Sell process will take as long as it must. It is guaranteed that if you do follow the Buy/Sell process, you can control the deal since you have the tools to be in control. The bottom line is that you will close more deals using a process. They will close faster, you will be in control, and you will avoid Maybeland.

Here are some general guidelines for this implementation phase of the process.

1. Stay longer in the early steps of the Buy/Sell process. Use the Educate process to make sure your product fit and qualification questions are answered. Remember, education is a two-way process. Spend a good amount of time educating the prospect and you'll discover that you understand the prospect's questions at a much deeper (and therefore more useful) level. Then you can use the Validate step to reinforce the education process, rather than using the Validate step to Educate. This is a common mistake. The longer you stay in the education stage, the better off you are, so stay there as long as you think you need to, and don't have the prospect push you forward at a pace that will decrease your chances for a sale.

Once you pass the Education stage, the Buy/Sell process starts to take off, activity levels increase, and the prospect is starting to gear up for a decision. The more homework you have done, the better you can create value in the later part of the process.

2. Stay in control. Prospects are going to want to map out their process near the end of the sale and have you follow it, especially the more senior the executive, or the higher the dollar value of the sale. The closer to the end you are, the greater the pressure for control of the process. You need to avoid the reactive selling mistake: As you get closer to the end of a sale, you end up thinking, *"If I do what the prospect is asking for, I'll get the sale."*

As you learned in Chapter 1, a valid business reason will help you stay in control—not obedience to the prospect's wishes.

3. Know when you have a qualified deal. Unless the MMM questions are answered, you should not be going past the Education stage. If you're entering the Validate phase, and you still have four of the seven MMM questions unanswered, Maybeland is coming up really fast. As we stressed in Chapter 9, if you master the seven questions of

MMM, you will do more to affect your income than anything else covered in this book.

4. Use your tools and create new behaviors! Twenty-five qualification questions, or pages and pages of diagrams and organizational maps, serve only one purpose: They keep you busy doing internal instead of external activities. You need to concentrate instead on external activities and keep prospecting. Now there's a new behavior for you. Call on more Russians than Spaniards . . . another new behavior. It just takes confidence and use of the tools.

The Fourth Step: Get Them Involved

Now comes the fun part. Many ProActive salespeople share their homework or at least the Buy/Sell process with the prospect. It works very well with Spaniards, and when you call on a Russian or a Greek, "sharing the process" acts as a tool that keeps you in control of that sales call as well. Since it is all about them, they get very interested.

Get creative with your Spaniards. Give them homework assignments along the way (the Gives/Gets^{Tool}, remember that one?). And speaking of "Gets," remember the GETS Chart? Have GETS meetings, which will include discussions of the SalesMap and the MMM questions. This is a great way to have progress reports and to ensure that both parties are still involved. It helps with the transfer of ownership, and every so often, you can invite a Russian to sit in.

The Fifth Step: Share with Others

If want to get really good at the tools in *ProActive Selling*, teach. Share what you do and what you are going to do with others. Share your current ideas, and put them together in a 15-minute presentation. What tools are you using, and how are you customizing the tools to use them better? There are four levels of salespeople.

At the first level is the rookie salesperson, the one just starting out. At the second level is the salesperson who has been around for a few years, has some experience, has been through some training, and has had some successes and failures. Third-level salespeople are very good. They are the ones who are very perceptive, based on their knowledge, experience, and talents. Most top sales leaders in organizations are perceptive salespeople.

At the very top are the fourth-level salespeople. They are the ones who can teach. They understand what they do so well and have taken ownership of the tools they use so well that they can teach them to others. This fourth-level salesperson has the confidence to go into almost any situation and come out winning, because they have a clear mastery of selling tools. They got that mastery by teaching others.

The same holds true with the tools in *ProActive Selling*. Once a week, once a month, seek out someone and tell that person how you are using a tool, or how you are going to use one, and why. Don't make the mistake of explaining how you used a tool. Discussions of past successes (and failures) are great, but in teaching the tools, you want to put yourself out there and discuss the unknown, current deals you can affect. History discussions can be used to validate the education of the selling tools. Use current discussions to teach; use examples from the past to have the learning really sink in.

Teach the tools, share them with others, and you'll find yourself taking ownership of these tools and developing new tools that are tailored to your own situation. You probably need more tools in your toolbox than just your current hammer and drill anyway, and if you can share your new tools with others, you will become a master at using them.

The Three Languages

Over and over, the three languages concept is the one salespeople really get an *ah-ha!* from. Salespeople understand they need to call high and stay high. The problem is their company is only putting out Feature/ Function sales and marketing tools for them to use. Marketing collateral, demos, proposals, trade shows, selling tools, everything is designed for a salesperson to master Feature/ Function selling. When salespeople get together, their common language is Spanish. Sales account reviews done with sales management are also done in Spanish. Everyone has a common language, Spanish. There's just too much Spanish.

You can, of course, tell the marketing department as well as all departments about the three languages and the need for more selling assistance to speak in terms of value (Russian and Greek). You probably should do this to effect change. Instead of throwing grenades at everyone else, you can do something yourself. Teach them. You can take the initiative, master the languages, and help the organization speak all three. Tips for getting better at the three languages include the following:

1. Call on current customers. Talk to the CFO, VP of Sales, or other executives within your current customers' organizations. Since you are currently a vendor, they will usually grant you some time, as long as there's something in it for them. Talk to them about how your product or service is working in their account, and ask for their opinion on how they could be using it better, to maximize their ROI. Get the meeting and listen; *do not pitch.* This is not selling time; this is learning-a-language time. You can use what you will be learning later. Remember, if you are getting a meeting to learn a new language, say Russian, and in return you converse with the executive in Spanish, the chances of you getting any more meetings with this Russian are slim to none. Learn a language, try to talk back to the executive in the same language, and leave the sales pitch back at the office.

2. Do your homework. There are important things you should be reading: outside periodicals, prospects' financial statements, the *Wall Street Journal*, annual reports, the financial section of the prospect's website, and so on. And yes, they're all in Russian and Greek, so you'll be gaining fluency as well as information. Become a student of Value—their values. You know you are becoming successful when your desk has financial reports and documents about your prospect's business rather than your own marketing collateral.

3. Prospect high. Develop a 30-Second Speech for upper-level management—in Russian. Then prepare one in Greek.

It seems that 90+ percent of salespeople say that they want to call high in an organization. They are being told to, and they do, but then they have an expectation of being passed down to a manager. It is acceptable to the reactive salesperson to be passed down.

> "The top executive told me what to do, and now I can reference the top executive when I call the lower-level person. They will have to take my call."

But it's not acceptable to the ProActive salesperson. We obliterated this attitude in Chapter 1. The two things that need to be fixed in this scenario are:

◆ Change the paradigm. Reward yourself for successful senior management calls differently than for manager calls. It cannot be an acceptable practice for you to be passed down. It should make you angry, since you now know what to say to senior management.

♦ Change the 30-Second Speech. Most 30-Second Speeches are focused on what the seller can offer the buyer. Remember, buyers don't care about you; they care about themselves. Prospect with WIIFM in the 30-Second Speech—and do it in the right language.

4. Stay the course. Keep working at mastering all languages, and you'll find yourself becoming multilingual. Homework you do will now appear to you in a multilingual format. Homework is always presented in multiple languages; you just have to learn how to read in a multilingual way.

Here's a good example of a multilingual story. Read the following fictitious newspaper article. See how it is written in three languages, and watch how your interest shifts.

Layoffs in the Recording Industry

LOS ANGELES—Struggling music power Tip-Top Records said yesterday that it will slash about 30 percent of its nearly 7,200-person workforce and dump about 200 acts from its roster in an effort to improve profits during an industrywide slump.

"There are some real challenges facing the music industry at the moment," Tip-Top CEO Jim Bertram says. "However, we are firmly on target to improve Tip-Top's performance, and we are optimistic about our ability to attack larger issues."

Spanish introduction ↓

Tip-Top—whose hitmakers include Steve W., John Brown, and superstar Christina M.—has been hurt as U.S. album sales in 2001 fell nearly 5 percent.

Some Spanish and Russian mixed in. Still holds your interest. ↓

Tip-Top's market share slid when it didn't have a hit to rival its release in late 2000 of *The Early Rock and Roll Days.* Superstar Gordon Loss failed to sparkle when his album *Funny* ended up selling only 400,000 copies. In January the company agreed to pay him $35 million to end their four-album contract.

Good Spanish, focused on industry gossip. ↓

Tip-Top is the No. 6 record company in the United States, with 11.3 percent of album sales so far in 2002, down from 14.2 percent in the same period last year, according to Soundscan.

In search of a turnaround, Tip-Top in October recruited Bertram, who had spiffed up Capital before Bertelsmann bought it in 1999.

Here comes the real Russian and Greek. ↓

Now, Bertram predicts higher market share and better cash flow margins as Tip-Top cuts costs, embraces new distribution technology, including DVDs and the Web, and attacks piracy.

The cuts should save $130 million a year by 2005, he says, and margins could grow in three years to 12 percent from the 2.1 percent expected this year.

Bertram will focus on marketing Tip-Top's best-known labels, DeLux and GoldOne. "Not having star power tends to take the margins out of the music and makes it a commodity," he told analysts in Los Angeles. That's one reason Tip-Top plans to drop more acts. "We've cut the artist roster a lot, but it was still pretty bloated," he says.

Several analysts were impressed with the changes. "The size of the cost savings beat our expectations, and the margin improvement is ahead of what we were looking for," says CreditSwiss analyst Hank Bush. "It's the turnaround story of the media sector." Still, Merrill Lynch's Ron Lewis says Tip-Top's ability to achieve its cash-flow goals "depends on a recovery (in music) and breaking more acts in the United States. But the team they put together is very compelling."

Tip-Top shares were up nearly 3 percent in U.S. trading.

Learn to read and understand all languages. The news article above is an example of how you have to focus on all languages in a story, not just what makes the headlines. It might be more interesting to read and talk Spanish, but Russians and Greeks make the decisions.

The Final Word

Sales is one part company, one part product, and one part you. You represent the company and its products, as well as the company's potential success. More than that, you also represent the prospects and clients you work for. It's up to you to help them change and do it profitably so they can continue to grow. They are asking for your help, so help them.

ProActive Selling was written for those who treat selling as a profession with integrity. That means you are responsible to be the best you can be. You are responsible for learning, growing, and changing too. The tools were developed for you to do just that. Thanks for reading this book. Use the tools!

Appendix: *ProActive Selling* Tools

Here are the tools in a single-page format. Copy this page and put it up in your office. It will remind you of what you should be preparing for on every call.

Ask 'em/Tell 'em/Ask 'em[Tool](Chapter 7)

BBB—Buyers Buy Backwards[Tool](Chapter 9)

Cause/Effect[Tool](Chapter 2)

CliffDive[Tool](Chapter 11)

Drop/Pull/Push[Tool](Chapter 11)

Feature/Benefit/Value[Tool](Chapter 2)

Finding Trains[Tool](Chapter 8)

Flip[Tool](Chapter 5)

GAP Chart[Tool](Chapter 7)

Gives/Gets[Tool](Chapter 10)

Implementation Date[Tool](Chapter 9)

Implementation Plan[Tool](Chapter 11)

PPPII[Tool](Chapter 9)

SalesMap[Tool](Chapter 7)

Summarize, Bridge, Pull[Tool](Chapter 5)

Solution Box[Tool] (Chapter 8)

STT—Short-Term Transfer[Tool] (Chapter 11)

30-Second Speech[Tool] (Chapter 5)

30-Second Speech: Second Call and Beyond[Tool](Chapter 6)

Three Languages[Tool](Chapter 3)

Three Levels of Why[Tool](Chapter 9)

TimeDemo[Tool] (Chapter 10)

TimeZones[Tool] (Chapter 3)

TOWARDS/AWAY[Tool] (Chapter 1)

20-Second Help Speech[Tool](Chapter 6)

20-Second Pattern Interrupt Speech[Tool] (Chapter 6)

ValueStar[Tool] (Chapter 3)

Index